IN CHARGE

IN CHARGE

FINDING THE
LEADER
WITHIN YOU

Myles Munroe

New York   Boston   Nashville

Unless otherwise noted, Scripture quotations are from the HOLY BIBLE: NEW INTERNATIONAL VERSION®, NIV®, © 1973, 1978, 1984 by the International Bible Society. Used by permission of Zondervan. All rights reserved. Scripture quotations marked (kjv) are taken from the King James Version of the Holy Bible. Scripture quotations marked (nkjv) are taken from the NEW KING JAMES VERSION, © 1979, 1980, 1982, by Thomas Nelson, Inc. Used by permission. All rights reserved. Scripture quotations and source information have sometimes been set italic for author's emphasis.

FaithWords

Hachette Book Group

237 Park Avenue

New York, NY 10017

Visit our Web site at www.faithwords.com.

Printed in the United States of America

First Edition: November 2008

10 9 8 7 6 5 4 3 2 1

FaithWords is a division of Hachette Book Group, Inc.
The FaithWords name and logo are trademarks of Hachette Book Group, Inc.

Library of Congress Cataloging-in-Publication Data

Munroe, Myles.
In charge : finding the leader within you / Myles Munroe.
p. cm.
ISBN-13: 978-0-446-58046-5
1. Leadership. 2. Leadership—Religious aspects—Christianity.
3. Self-actualization (Psychology). I. Title.
HD57.7.M862 2008
658.4'092—dc22
2008017646

To the 6.7 billion people on earth searching for meaning and significance in life, believing deep inside that they were born to do more than survive, make a living and die.

To the individual stuck in the human rat race and imprisoned by the notion that success in life is the accumulation of material things. My hope is that you be set free from the cycle of futility in pursuing goals set in life by your culture and society and discover the secret to your personal fulfillment.

To the youth of our nations who seek purpose and meaning in life. May you discover the value and power of your inherent gift and become a leader in your generation by serving that gift to the world.

To all the trustees and members of the International Third World Leaders Association! May you continue to manifest and maximize the leadership capacity in you and others.

To my son and daughter, Charisa and Chairo (Myles Jr.), who's leadership potential inspired many of the principles in this work. May you continue to follow your destiny to serve your leadership gift to your generation.

To the Source of all true gifts, the Creator of destinies and Sustainer of life. May your truth explode in the hearts of all who read these pages.

ACKNOWLEDGMENTS

Every accomplishment in life is the result of corporate effort. Just as it takes a village to raise a child, so it takes a team to author a book. Being aware that we are all a sum total of all that we have learned from all the people and experiences we have met and had in our lives, no one can claim full credit of any measure of success in any endeavor. This book is no different.

I want to thank my beloved wife Ruth, and my children, Charisa and Chairo (Myles Jr.), for their support, patience and corporation while I pursue the many projects included in my earthly assignment. You are all my principle treasures. Thanks for helping me manifest my inherent gift and allowing me to serve it to the world.

Adrienne Ingram, who coordinated this project, for encouragement, input, dedication, motivation and continued pursuit of me in getting this project done.

Angela Dodson for your incredible gift, inspiration and skill in bringing the best of this content out of me. This work could not have been completed without you as you continually and consistently demonstrated the very principle in this book—servant leadership. I am eternally grateful and will always remember your contribution through your gift.

CONTENTS

PART 2

THE SEVEN PRINCIPLES OF SERVANT LEADERSHIP

PART 3

PREPARED TO SERVE

THE PRACTICE OF LEADERSHIP

Taught to Serve, Not to Lead

It was a beautiful sun-drenched morning in my village called Bain's Town on the little island twenty miles long and seven miles wide called New Providence, also home of our capital, Nassau. Over two hundred of us, just six and seven years old, stood outside on the hard dirt ground, wearing our neatly pressed green and white school uniforms. Each of us held a twelve-inch stick to which was attached a cloth print of the Flag of the United Kingdom of Great Britain, called the Union Jack. At nine o'clock in the morning, the temperature was already ninety degrees, but we were commanded to not move a muscle. Droplets of perspiration fell from my brow and into my mouth. It was Commonwealth-Flag Day, and we were keeping a long-standing tradition of our imperial rulers.

All over the island, every school was mandated to gather all students in assemblies to honor the Queen of Great Britain through patriotic songs, recitations of British poetry and corporate pledges to our monarch and the empire for which they stood. We were all called colonies and knew we were considered second-class subjects of Her Majesty and the Great United Kingdom of Great Britain.

I was participating in the same ceremony as countless millions of others throughout the commonwealth of Great Britain. We were all subjects of "colonies" of European kingdoms. These kingdoms included Great Britain, France, Spain, Portugal, Belgium and Holland. Colonization impacted most of the world, including Central and South America, Africa, India, the Pacific Islands, Asia, North America, and the Caribbean Islands, where I was born.

On that hot Commonwealth Day morning under that scorching, uncovered sun, we sang the songs of the Empire, as we did every morning. As uniformed children, we enjoyed singing these songs, each of us straining to be heard above the others. I did not know the mental impact of these imperial psalms. They were brainwashing, converting, conditioning and eventually shaping the self-concept, self-worth, self-esteem, and perception of the world in which we would live. These songs also reinforced the books used in each classroom by our British teachers, volumes that only spoke of the English life, culture and history. We were to be convinced that all that was British was good, and honorable, superior, and just.

However, the most vile impression on our young minds was that we were born to serve and worship the empire, that we were not capable of leadership. We were conditioned to "depend" on the colonial powers for life and value, trained that we could not determine our own destinies, chart our own future, plan our lives.

The precepts we, and those in colonies on every continent, were taught from the cradle throughout the entire span of life still affect us this very day in our post-colonial era. Here are words of songs we were made to sing every day; keep in mind that these were sung by the offspring of those who had been enslaved:

When Britain first at Heav'n's command
Arose from out the azure main;
Arose, arose from out the azure main;
This was the charter, the charter of the land,
And guardian angels sang this strain:

Rule, Britannia! Britannia, rule the waves!
Britons never, never, never shall be slaves!
Rule, Britannia! Britannia, rule the waves!
Britons never, never, never shall be slaves!

Or the favorite one:

God save our gracious Queen
Long live our noble Queen
God save the Queen!
Send her victorious,
Happy and glorious,
Long to reign over us,
God save the Queen!

The statements that had the greatest impact on our impressionable minds were: "Britons never, never, never shall be slaves" and "Long to reign over us."

These songs were sung by millions in the colonies of Africa, Asia, the Americas, and the Caribbean. We sang both of these statements while we were slaves and subjects of the imperial powers. "*They* would never be slaves" while we were enslaved at the time we sang. Can you imagine the psychological implications?

The results of this experience was independent nations led by and composed of peoples who were robbed of their sense of self, self-worth, self-confidence, and belief in their abilities to lead. Most nations that are products of this colonization–mental conditioning have struggled and continue to struggle with the leadership issues.

It is ironic that the former colonizers and imperial powers blame and accuse these new, developing nations for their lack of effective leadership, when in fact they created the poor leaders who often govern these nations.

Colonization and imperial oppression throughout history resulted in the failure to mentor, develop, cultivate, and produce leaders. The oppression that permeated the American society had the same result. The Founding Fathers of America were products of the society that perpetrated colonization and the philosophy of superiority through domination. Hence, the slave trade thrived in the early years of the Federation of the United States of America, and the formally oppressed peoples of the American society—such as the American Indians and the Negro slaves—struggle today with the issue of effective leadership development in their communities.

Oppression never produces leadership but suffocates the great leadership potential that resides in every human.

My Journey of Discovery

From this context, I emerged to face life and grapple with the internal need to find significance. The mental conditioning that I was "born to be ruled" and destined by providence to be a "slave" were my opposing forces. When I was young, I had no idea that this was a psychological oppression practiced as far back as the Egyptian civilization that permeated the empires of the Greeks and Romans, and became the thread running through the fabric of the colonial tapestry of the so-called New World.

So standing there in the heat of the Caribbean sun, I was beginning a journey to discover that I was not "born to be ruled" nor destined to be a follower trapped by providence to a life of subjugation.

It took years for my mind to be delivered from the historical damage of oppression and to understand not only that I was capable of becoming a leader, and destined to be one, but also that *every* human on this planet was created for the purpose of leadership and possessed leadership capacity and potential. This book is about that discovery. It's about you and the potential you possess to become an influence in your world and future generations.

True leadership does not maintain followers but produces leaders. That is what this book is about. I will address this historical scar on the psyche of the human race and provide the insight, tools and understanding necessary to free each individual from the shackles of oppression. I want to challenge and dare you, as an aspiring leader, to discover the truth about leadership that no human can cancel if you embrace it.

Questions from the Heart

*I*s leadership about power, position, talent, skill, authority, some unique physical trait, social status, family heritage, or special charisma? Is leadership a product of birth privilege or the result of casting lots or a democratic vote? Is leadership a corporate appointment or the reward bestowed after a struggle with competitive forces? Is leadership reserved for just an elite few chosen by providence and separated from the masses of us normal mortals who struggle for a sense of significance?

Does leadership require followers? Is it necessary for leaders to have titles? Is leadership a distinction of superiority, a disposition of advantage and qualities of greatness that separate one from the rest? Is leadership a manifestation of superior intellect or cognitive capacity? Is leadership reserved only to a specific race or class of people? Are leaders smarter, wiser, better, greater, more intelligent, more equipped, more skillful, and more charismatic than followers are?

These are questions I struggled with from my youth growing up in my native Caribbean home of the Bahamas, and I believe I have found the answers.

*   *   *

Nothing happens without leadership. Nothing changes without leadership. Nothing develops without leadership. Nothing improves without leadership. Nothing is corrected without leadership. Everyone, everywhere, every time is always being led. Whatever conditions, circumstances or predicament in which a person, family, community, organization or nation may find itself, someone led it there.

We are always, directly or indirectly, consciously or unconscientiously, being led. Leadership is perpetually exercised over us, whether by a politician, priest, parent, boss or teacher. Even the blind can lead, according to the young Jewish rabbi Jesus Christ.

It is said that we all get the leaders we deserve. In essence, we are usually led by the persons to whom we choose to submit ourselves whether by vote, choice, or agreement.

Of all the challenges our twenty-first-century world must confront, such as terrorism, wars, epidemics, global warming, and corporate corruption, the greatest challenge is finding effective leaders. Europeans are looking for leaders to address immigration and economic concerns. Former Soviet nations are looking for leaders to solve business production and crime issues. African countries are looking for leadership that will end the culture of corruption and end civil war and other dire crises such as drought, famine, and AIDS. Emerging nations, such as Iraq, hope for leadership that will adequately represent the various factions and needs in their country.

Many Leaders, Little Leadership

It is not that we do not have people occupying offices of leadership in our world. We have many leaders today—but, sadly, not much leadership. We have leaders in social, religious, political, and other arenas, but what kind of world have all these leaders and their predecessors produced?

Our world is dealing with crucial issues that must be addressed.

Our global conditions *demand* good leadership. Yet our dilemma is that either leaders have helped to create these problems, or they are overwhelmed by the problems they have inherited. Every dire condition of humanity is the result of poor leadership.

For example, technological advancement is outpacing culture. Only about 10 percent of the world's population has access to technology that can improve and even save lives, which means we are isolating billions of people from advancement. Yet, at the same time, nations that have access to the latest technology are being "advanced" beyond their abilities to keep pace with all the developments. Change is occurring so rapidly that people cannot absorb and apply it in their lives in a healthy way. So-called conveniences of communication and business have become a burden, rather than the benefit that technology leaders envisioned.

Another problem is unequal distribution of the earth's resources. Poverty, per se, does not exist in the world. It is caused largely by a leadership problem that does not allow the earth's resources to go to those who need them.

I was in Minnesota to conduct seminars and appear on some television programs. During my time there, my host drove me to Fargo, North Dakota. You can drive for three or four hours in that region, and all you see is beautiful farmland.

My host asked me, "Do you see the corn? The reason why they are not harvesting it, even though it is ready, is that the price is not right yet. And if the price is not right, they will destroy that corn and fold it back into the ground so they can create a shortage."

People in Zambia, Malawi, and Botswana need corn, but because the price is not right, farmers in North Dakota destroy it rather than ship it to Africa.

When food *is* sent to poor countries, distribution problems often keep it from getting to those who need it most. Some of those countries' leaders will store the food for themselves and let their own people go hungry. There is no real poverty in the world; rather, there are political, business, and investment leaders who are motivated by other agendas.

Then there are international health issues. Every sixty seconds, seven people contract AIDS. The health threat is unimaginable, and our medical leaders seem helpless to address it.

There are religious and cultural clashes. When I was in England recently, they were debating what to do about the Muslim communities because some British citizens of Muslim descent were organizing and plotting to destroy the country. When your own citizens become terrorists based on religious differences, you have a national leadership problem.

Similarly, France is grappling with the growing influx of Muslims from Turkey. They are afraid they have to change the school system to accommodate Islamic clothing and language. Government leaders do not know what to do with the educational system because immigration seems to be shaking its foundation.

The United States is facing its own immigration issues. Some debate whether or not to build a wall along its border with Mexico. At the same time, many congressional leaders fight for immigrants to receive status and privileges.

These are all leadership dilemmas.

Family disintegration is another issue. Fifty-one percent of the children in American and other Western society's classrooms come from families without fathers. We have dysfunctional families that are expected to produce citizens who can function in society. When these children are sent to school, things become chaotic because they do not know what it means to respect authority. They lack parental leadership in the home.

Inadequate leadership has also led us to an era of confused sexual orientation. When those who are making the laws are not sure if marriage should be between a man and a woman, a lack of leadership is evident. We have leaders challenging the ideal structure of the traditional family, and the very definition of family is being debated. When two men or two women who are in a sexual relationship can adopt a baby, this reflects a challenge in leadership.

These are all leadership dilemmas.

The Human Condition

As a result of this void of effective, competent leadership, many people have developed destructive attitudes and perspectives that dominate their lives.

Fear. People are afraid of terrorism, ethnic clashes, disasters, war, disease, and economic collapse. This is the real world in which we live. I was in Oklahoma City when the bombing took place. The problem of terrorism—homegrown or international—was real in Oklahoma and New York City, and it is real all over the world.

Disillusionment. People are losing hope for their lives. For example, some young people are wondering, "Why should I finish school or start a career when I can sell drugs and buy whatever I want?" Older people are wondering why they should tell the truth on their tax forms or keep their integrity at work.

Anger. People are angry about their inabilities to deal with their lives. A growing bitterness pervades the world, and it spills over into domestic violence, road rage and racial strife. Young people are angry with their parents who were not there for them, or who would not show them love and discipline. Then they take their bitterness out on society through destructive lifestyles and actions.

Distrust. A spirit of distrust and suspicion is growing. People are weary of broken promises in government, dishonest business practices, and unfaithfulness in the home.

Compromise. People who are distrustful and bitter find it easier to compromise their values and morals to try to get by in life. They may sleep with the boss for advancement or with the teacher to get good grades. They may steal from their employers if they do not feel they are paid enough.

Selfishness. Our leaders have encouraged a self-centered environment. People are tempted to ignore others around them, and even those in need look out only for themselves. Certain lawyers will list a myriad of reasons and ways you can sue people just to get some money.

Over-competitiveness. People believe there are not enough resources to go around, so they compete with others, rather than cooperate.

Covetousness or greed. People are flooded with material goods and advertisements for these goods, so they begin to covet things they cannot afford. If a teenager cannot buy Nike shoes, he beats up someone who can and takes them. If a man cannot afford to buy the same kind of car his co-worker has, he uses his children's tuition money to buy it. If a family does not have the money for a vacation or a wide-screen television, they purchase on credit.

Devaluation of life. This issue is dangerous because when human life is devalued, it signals the demise of a society. When the termination of unborn babies is considered legal, then human life is considered to be of no consequence. Yet abortion is considered an option whenever it's "inconvenient" to have a baby. Euthanasia and assisted suicide are gaining proponents.

Abuse. Parents are abusing children through violence and incest. Husbands are beating their wives because, for various reasons, these men feel worthless. Wives stay in these situations because they also feel worthless.

Violence. We live on a violent planet. Although the United States is the leading democracy in the world, it has the highest number of homicides among the nations. More murders take place in Washington, D.C., the seat of government, than in any other place in the country.

In the Middle East, the daily suicide bombings that kill innocent adults and children are becoming such a common occurrence that it is now just another footnote on the daily serving of news reports. The abuse, rape, and killings of refugees in developing nations baffle the imagination.

War. The world is at war. There is war in our homes between husbands and wives or children and parents, war in our schools between students and teachers, war in our businesses between managers and staff, war in our churches between members and pastors, wars between religions and sects, and war between our nations. Innocent bystanders of these wars suffer the most.

We need to understand that the state of the world described above is the product of leadership throughout history. Our global, national and community conditions are simply proof that the nature, quality, and characteristics of leadership mankind has produced over the years have not served us well. A vacuum exists—lack of proper, effective, efficient, spiritually sensitive, genuine leadership—on all levels.

Yet here is the catch: our leaders come from among ourselves. Our cultures produce inadequate leaders and breed problems that leadership cannot fix, which generates further problems that new leaders cannot address. There is a principle of life, "Everything produces after its kind." You cannot produce something better than yourself. Perhaps that is why the leaders we continue to produce throughout generations do not improve nor can they bring improvement.

Everyone Wants to Be a Leader!

Politicians fight for it, clergy jockey for it, athletes abuse drugs for it, businesspeople compromise for it, competitors scheme for it, and students cheat for it. Yet few would admit their deep aspiration to leadership. This secret desire for leadership is inherent in the human spirit.

The search for leaders to fill the vacuum causes us to ask the question, What does it mean to be a leader? What qualities should we be looking for in the ideal leader?

Why Is Leadership Failing?

Traditionally, leaders have been trained in schools of business and government. Yet something must be lacking in these institutions and their teachings if their graduates are unable to address crucial leadership issues or exhibit genuine leadership qualities.

Despite the fact that leadership in all areas of society seems to be falling short, and trustworthy leaders are in short supply, the desire for the perfect leader is still a deep desire in us all. However, no matter how we try, our leaders continue to fall short of our expectations. The failure of leadership today is two-edged: (1) People's inability to lead creates and perpetuates poor human conditions. (2) The failure of leadership does not allow for the emergence of much-needed leadership development in the majority of the people in the world who are considered mere "followers."

Would-be emerging leaders are squelched before they have an opportunity to develop. The process of mentoring leaders through training and coaching is gravely lacking. This is a tragedy for individuals, their families, communities, nations, and the world that cannot benefit from effective competent leadership.

Yet when you understand what it means to become a true leader, you can begin to address the problems in the world, because you will be free from the mind-sets and practices that prevent true leadership and keep people defeated. You cannot lead if you are trapped by the followers.

I believe it is possible to find leadership that can improve the lot of humanity. We can each be an example of that perfect leader we all desire.

PART 1

DESTINED TO SERVE AND LEAD

THE PARADOX

1

"I'm In Charge": The Battery and the Wire

WHO'S GOT THE POWER?

"The value in each human is the gift they were born to deliver to humanity."

Which one of these is the most important part of a car: the battery or the terminal wire? You've probably never heard of the little red wire that connects the battery to the rest of the engine in the car. If you're like most people you will say, "The battery. It has the power."

Your car has about 60,000 parts. The battery says, "I'm in charge of all of them. Nothing starts without me. I'm the battery. I have the power. Power! Power! Power! I'm the one who starts everything. Nothing starts until I arrive. I'm the power. I've got the power to start the engine."

Does that sound like some people you know?

Well, if the battery is the most important part of the car, let's disconnect the wire. The battery costs about $150. The little red wire missing from the car costs about $10. You have 59,999 working parts and only a $10 wire missing. Without it, the car will not start. Your car may be worth $40,000, $50,000 or $100,000, but it can be immobilized by this

$10 wire. You want to go somewhere. You have something to do! The car says, "I'm ready, but there's a little $10 wire missing."

The battery says, "I've got the power."

A spark plug says, "I've got the fire."

The engine says, "I run the car!"

That little wire is very quiet. He does not have to say, "You need me. You can't start without me." All the other parts soon realize it, and they say, "Go find the wire." The terminal wire was created to transmit electrical current from the battery to the generator and to the engine to ignite the spark plugs that provide the fire to turn the pistons and turn the engine over. In essence, the little terminal wire was designed to be the "leader" in the area of electrical transmission. In the domain of the terminal wire, the terminal wire is in charge. It might be just a little wire, but it could shut down the engine.

If that spot is empty, the car shuts down.

Each one of the car's parts is a leader. A spark plug can never be a battery. A battery can never be a manifold. A manifold can never be a generator. Therefore, in the domain of the battery, the battery is in charge. It is unique because only it can be the battery—no matter how jealous the battery or the spark plug gets, no matter how much the steering wheel wishes to be a battery.

Each part is important. Every component of the car was designed to lead in a specific area and to serve a purpose or function in the context of the whole. Each one is a leader!

This concept of leadership contradicts the philosophy that leadership is reserved for a small, elite group of individuals "chosen by providence" and entitled to lead the masses of incapable subordinates in need of guidance by those of superior status. It is a direct challenge to what I was taught in the colonial experience of my childhood.

My view of leadership is this: each of us has an inherent gift and must serve that gift to the world. You are a leader. You have power. Your gift is your power. You are in charge in your area of gifting, your domain. You have a leadership spot to fill and a function to carry out. Your gift determines that spot and that function. Just as the value of the terminal wire is determined not by size or cost but by function, your value is not determined by anything but your gift. Someone needs your gift, and you must serve it to the world. You also need the gifts others bear to live.

So who's in charge? You are! Who's got the power? Every one of us.

2

Born to Lead, Prepared to Serve

SERVING YOUR WAY TO LEADERSHIP

"The desire not to be anything is the desire not to be."
—Ayn Rand

You are a leader. You were created to lead. You have leadership potential. Trapped within you is a hidden leader.

If your first reaction is to say, "Oh, no! Not me," you are not alone. The vast majority do not believe that they are leaders, have leadership ability or could even achieve leadership positions. All cultures devalue humanity in some way, and this mental conditioning is the result in even the best circumstances. The brainwashing I shared in the Foreword is among the worst, but few recognize their God-given leadership.

When I encounter people who think they cannot be leaders, I tell them that they can, they *must* and they should, because they owe it to their generation. You have to start believing you are a leader.

Each person is like a star in the galaxy. You have your own radiance, but the traditions and conventions of man have told you that you have no light. The cultures of oppression have snuffed out the belief that you can lead in an area of gifting.

A leader is born when you discover your gift. Finding out what excites you and consumes you, discovering your passion, helps to determine your gift. This requires a process of self-discovery. How will you know what your gift is? Here are some clues: Your gift is fun. You enjoy it, you can do it all day, and people will even pay you to do what you like to do. It is your passion. You could do it without pay, 24/7 for 365 days of the year.

Leadership consists of finding, refining and passing on one's unique gift—that "brand" only you have. If you refine your gift, develop your gift, and then serve your gift to the world, you become great.

True leaders never retire, because you cannot retire from yourself. When you are known for your gift, the world will come to you for it.

My passion is leadership. I have devoted much of my life, thousands and thousands of hours, to the study of leadership, listening to and reading the ideas of experts on business and economics and philosophy but ultimately finding the answer in servant leadership.

I live to teach and to share ideas that make people discover who they are, what their value is, what their worth is, what they can do, what they can achieve and what they can become. To me, the ultimate we can do for our fellow humans is to help them become the best they can become and to have a life where they can do more with their gifts.

I became fascinated with leadership early in life and began studying it while earning degrees in education, fine arts, and theology from Oral Roberts University and a master's degree in leadership administration from the University of Tulsa. I had considered studying in London, as many people in my country do because we were a British colony, but I had heard of this Christian university and wanted to go there. As a freshman, I was appointed to a committee that met with the president of the college every week. As a result, I was able to observe and learn directly from Oral Roberts, who founded the university in Tulsa, Oklahoma, in 1963 and remains chancellor.

Roberts is one of the greatest examples of servant-leadership living. I do not believe a day went by that I did not hear the word *heal* come out of his mouth. Healing is his passion. He lives and works out his dream, his vision and his gift for the benefit of so many millions of people. His desire to improve the lives of people is the motivation for everything he does. He has passion and compassion in perfect balance. This is what leadership really is.

Leadership is passion, but it must also be balanced by the sensitivity and the desire to see people's lives healed, improved and developed. That is the compassion component. Because of that passion and compassion, he is constantly trying to find as many ways as possible to serve the needs of the people. That was the example I saw in him.

For me, born as the middle child in a family of eleven in one of the poorest areas of the Bahamas, I was also inspired by the way that Roberts, who was part Cherokee and from a family of modest means, had overcome obstacles to become a great leader. I was able to observe and learn from a mentor who had achieved against the odds. He would tell me, "Dream no small dreams around here, because nothing is impossible."

A Firm Foundation

When I went on for my graduate degree, I studied all the theories about leadership. I thought, "Something is wrong with these theories, but I will study them anyway." When I returned home after my studies, I went to work for the government and continued studying leadership.

My parents had introduced me to the Scriptures early in life. My father, Mathias, a lay minister, and mother, Louise, a community volunteer, also provided outstanding examples of unselfish service to others, always feeding others and sharing what little we had.

The Bible instilled in me a sense of self-worth to counter the low expectations society had for us under colonialism before the Bahamas became independent. I began my public ministry around age 15, sharing ideas about the value of humans, based on my understanding of the lifestyle of Jesus Christ. My ministry was partly an outgrowth of my role in a music group that was known all over the Bahamas.

As an adult, I started a Bible study that became a "church" of about seven members. It is now the largest church in the islands, Bahamas Faith Ministries International. Its work reaches 1.8 billion people in the world through direct ministry, books and broadcasts each week in more than eighty-seven countries. I have written numerous books that have been translated into twenty-one languages. I receive seven hundred to eight hundred invitations a year to speak and travel 250,000 miles a year. I have flown all over the world preaching, teaching, and sharing my ideas on leadership with churches, corporations, and governments.

My teacher, mentor, and coach is Jesus Christ, whom I believe taught the ultimate lessons on leadership through words and example. His idea is simple: to lead, you must serve.

Living to Serve

My father is also one of the best examples of servant leadership I have known. Not only did he and my mom work together to help others, but he also gave his whole life to serve our family, eleven children, and a wife. He served my mother for all fifty-one years of their marriage, and I was able to observe that.

Everything he did was to make us better. He never sought to do anything for himself. Being a lay minister in the church meant that he always wanted to serve outside the home as well. Today, even at age 83, he is still speaking in churches around the country and helping people.

He served in World War II. The British, who ruled our islands at the time, recruited many of the natives of African descent, the subjects, in an auxiliary to the Royal Air Force of the British Empire. They never saw any action, but apparently (RAF) worked to assist the aircrafts that were landing and taking off in the Bahamas. When the war ended, the British provided a contract of pension for their service.

My father is one of the last living members of that group and for the past ten years has served in a leadership position for them. Today, he is the appointed chairman. He keeps track of where the members are and takes the pension to them every week. It is just amazing to see him do it. He is driving around in a car, collecting their checks from the government, and finding where they live. Some of them live in the low-income areas of the island. He goes to them and makes sure that they get what they need and provides for them. He is 83 years old and still serving his comrades.

I sit back and just see a tremendous example of servant leadership—to never stop serving. He did not seek leadership. He just sought to serve people. Sometimes I ask him, "Where are you going? Why don't you rest?" He says, "I have got to go find my comrades and make sure they get their checks that they need to live. I need to take care of them." You would think he needs someone to take care of him, but he is the healthiest and most vibrant of them all. Maybe this is because he is serving them all.

Servant leadership is self-fulfilling, and he feels fulfilled in what he is doing. Everything is coming back to him as a harvest now.

First of All, Serve

"What is leadership?" It is, above all, service. A leader is a servant of the people. This is the teaching of Jesus Christ. How do you become a leader by serving? Simple, you have to serve something to the world. What do you serve? You serve your gift. When you find your gift and you serve it to the world, you become great. Jesus said greatness happens to you while you are serving your gift and because you are serving yourself to the world. Having others serve you does not make you great. Leadership has more to do with releasing yourself and deploying yourself, rather than employing people.

Whatever your gift in life is, it is not for you to keep; it is for you to give to the world. God gave it to you. Pass it on. Servant leadership is serving your gift at every opportunity. Servant leadership is serving yourself to the world. Servant leadership is self-distribution to your generation. Distributing yourself.

Servant leadership is being prepared to serve your gift at every opportunity. Stop waiting until you are great to start serving. Do not put it off until you get your degree, title, or promotion. Clean the bathroom and serve. Make tea and serve. Rearrange the chairs and serve. Run the cameras and serve. Sing in the choir and serve. Mow the lawn and serve. You serve at every opportunity.

If you want to become great, you first have to serve your gift without charge or compensation. Volunteer your service. I meet people barely out of school who want to charge fees for what they do. I do not understand this, but I tell them, "You can't even blow your sax well, and you want pay? You had better find a mentor who will even allow you to stand on the stage or carry the equipment."

3

Why Lead?

A WORLD IN NEED OF DIRECTION

"Never underestimate the power of One-self."

Not long ago, the security personnel made me loosen my belt at an airport for the first time in my life. I thought my pants would fall off. They said they wanted to make sure my buckle was not a knife. When my wife travels with me, she cannot even carry her personal toiletries on the plane. The fear is here. It is against this background of global convulsions that this international cry for competent, effective, capable, and spirit-filled leadership rises up. We need leaders now.

In Times Like These

Every week the media tells us about an election process somewhere as nations seek leaders who will better people's lives. Often this process produces a cadre of leaders on every continent, who continues to disappoint the voters and their communities with defective character, abuse of power, corruption, and a bankruptcy of ideas to address known problems. So the search for true leaders goes on. For example, every four years in the United States, two dozen presidential hopefuls begin the "political season" by declaring their candidacies for the highest elected office in the nation. That season has become longer and longer and the process more grueling with countless caucuses, primaries, campaign stops, and debates with scandals and meaningless backbiting along the way. Increasingly, it seems that no matter how many people run for this office, the citizens find it hard to name one worthy of their vote.

The United States is not alone in this problem. A void of leadership exists all over the world in both industrialized and developing nations. People wonder where they can find strong leaders they can trust.

Our government, military, businesses, schools, and churches need effective leaders who have the people's best interests at heart.

You must be one of those leaders, and you are now. In the darkest moments of despair, we have always looked to our leaders to take us through tough times. These include such biblical heroes as Moses, Joshua, Nehemiah, Esther, Deborah, David, and Daniel, and even such historic legends as Teddy Roosevelt, John F. Kennedy, and Sir Winston Churchill, who stirred a generation to believe that it could emerge from the Second World War. We had Martin Luther King Jr., Mahatma Gandhi, and Nelson Mandela to sound contemporary alarms for freedom and civil liberty.

Having visionary leaders—competent leadership, skillful leadership, and principal centered–leadership—is imperative. Most importantly, leadership today cannot look merely to human wisdom or intellect, to meet the challenges of our day. We need leadership. We need leadership that can tap into another world and into some other wisdom and some other solutions that we cannot invent on earth.

I believe that every need in the world would be met if everybody discovered and maximized the leadership potential within. Every human being was born to contribute to his or her generation. No one was given life to take up space. If everyone were to discover his or her own value, balanced by the understanding that everyone else has a contribution to make, all the needs in the world would be met.

It is my belief that every human need is a result of someone else not leading or not serving a gift to the world.

Everything rises and falls on leadership. So go the leaders, so goes the nation. So go the leaders, so goes the family. So go the leaders, so go our communities. If all of us serve our gifts to the world, we can improve our lives and others' lives. If all the parts work together, then humanity will run like a beautiful auto.

If we all become the leaders we were meant to be, we could solve many of the world's problems. But most people have not discovered who they are, what it is they have and how to serve it to the world. Servant leadership is a philosophy of leadership with a basic message:

Every human being was created to lead. Your desire and predisposition to lead is inborn.

Every human possesses leadership potential. You have the ability to lead in an area of gifting.

Trapped in every follower is a hidden leader. If you accept false ideas about who can or cannot become a leader, it can smother your potential.

Though everyone was born to lead, most will die as followers. If you do not identify and tap into your giftedness, it will be wasted and be buried with you.

Leadership is your history and your destiny. You were created to be a leader and designed to fulfill your assignment.

The world needs your leadership. You exist to meet a specific need on earth that no one else can meet.

4

Who Is the Greatest?

"THE ONE WHO SERVES"

"Every human came to earth with something humanity needs."

Everyone wants to play in the band—no one wants to just stand on stage or haul the equipment. Every human wants to be great! The desire for greatness is inherent in the human spirit and is a principal motivation for all human action and decisions. However, few would admit this reality, and most would deny it. Many parade their denial in a display of false humility claiming they only want to "serve," when in fact their motivation for service is attention, recognition, and admiration. In essence, self-serving is disguised as humility. Perhaps even the definition of greatness must be rediscovered and the traditional concept challenged, especially in our generation.

Greatness in our materialistic world is defined as fame, popularity, scholastic or economic achievement, and notoriety. Greatness may result from these qualities, but they are not the definition of greatness.

Greatness may best be defined by the people throughout history whom we consider great. Among those who would be considered great in the context of their influence and impact on human society are such names as Mother Teresa, Nelson Mandela, Abraham Lincoln, Martin Luther, Martin Luther King Jr., Michael Jordan, Tiger Woods, George Washington Carver, Thomas Edison, Benjamin Franklin, Mahatma Gandhi, Henry Ford, Bill Gates, Walt Disney, Alexander Graham Bell, Albert Einstein, Babe Ruth, Jesse Owens, Florence Nightingale, Helen Keller, Pablo Picasso, Sam Walton, Oprah Winfrey, Steven Spielberg, the Wright Brothers, Steven Jobs, and Bessie Coleman.

A careful study of each individual will reveal that greatness was not a product of academic studies or formal education, social status or superior breeding, but surprisingly the greatness of each was related to the discovery, development, refinement, and serving of a unique "gift" to their fellow men.

It is also essential to note that not one of them desired to be great or pursued greatness as a goal, but rather they were all preoccupied with pursuit of their unique gift in service to mankind. They were all possessed with an idea that would benefit humanity.

Greatness, therefore, has very little to do with the pursuit of popularity, fame, recognition, or power, but rather it is the result of "serving one's gift to the world."

When you serve your gift to the world you become significant to humanity and people will describe you as "great." In sum, greatness is significance. It comes from the value you bring to life with your gift. That is what this book is about, because every human on earth came with an inherent gift. That makes us all potentially great!

About two thousand years ago in a little village in the northern region of Israel, a young 30-year-old Jewish rabbi, who is considered the greatest human specimen that ever lived on earth, Jesus Christ, defined greatness to His students in this unique way. Let us review His class on greatness in leadership.

The Lesson in Capernaum

Traveling from Galilee to Capernaum one day, Jesus apparently overheard an argument among his students. When they arrived, He asked them about it. They grew silent, rather than admit to arguing about who was the greatest. Maybe He sensed it, because He immediately called all twelve together to explain His concept of greatness:

Mark 9:33–35
33 They came to Capernaum. When he was in the house, he asked them, "What were you arguing about on the road?"
34 But they kept quiet because on the way they had argued about who was the greatest.
35 Sitting down, Jesus called the Twelve and said, "If anyone wants to be first, he must be the very last, and the servant of all."

Scripture also says the students Jesus had around Him at His last Passover meal began to argue after He predicted one of them would betray Him:

Luke 22:24
Also a dispute arose among them as to which of them was considered to be greatest.

Once again, they were considering who was the greatest among them. "Who's the leader?" It was a leadership struggle. Jesus said to them, "The kings of the Gentiles Lord it over them [the people.]" (V. 25) He corrects them. He rebukes them. He does not rebuke their desires to be great. He rebukes the process they use.

Earlier, the disciples James and John had tried to achieve greatness by gaining advantage over others, by association, or inside information, or abuse of privilege, or violating friendship.

Matthew 20:20–21
20 Then the mother of Zebedee's sons came to Jesus with her sons and, kneeling down, asked a favor of him.

21 "What is it you want?" he asked. She said, "Grant that one of these two sons of mine may sit at your right and the other at your left in your kingdom."

They were trying to do what everyone does to get ahead. They were trying to become great at the expense of their friends, at the expense of the family they lived with for three years, at the expense of people who trusted them. They did not care about the other ten. The desire for greatness and position of leadership can cause people to sell their souls, violate their consciences, isolate their relationships, and abuse people's trust. That is what God rejects, not our desire for greatness.

The Creator of humankind is not against our grasp for greatness. God is against the process that people use to achieve it. Jesus did not discourage the desire for greatness. In fact, He encouraged the desire for it and showed the disciples how to achieve it. When His own men wanted to be great, He showed them *how* to become great. Jesus takes greatness and purifies it. Everyone on earth desires to be great, all of us, and Jesus says that desire is not ungodly.

"Who is the greatest?" is an eternal argument. Everybody wants to be the greatest. You want greatness, even if you do not admit it. Deep in the heart, everyone has a secret agenda to rise to the top. That is why we scheme. That is why we network and develop contacts, why we get an education and why we look for promotions. We want greatness. It is not just an ancient quest. It is still going on.

Moreover, we should be concerned when people do not want to be great. If your children or others in your environment do not desire greatness, something is wrong with them. They need attention. Someone has broken their spirit, discouraged them, or frustrated them. They have lost something. Anyone who swears they do not desire to be great is being dishonest.

The desire for greatness is sometimes defined or described as ambition, but this inherent desire is healthy for human development and feeds the human need for passion and pursuit. The desire for greatness is the source of purpose and inspires meaning. It gives the human spirit the motivation to aspire. The desire for greatness is where the incentive for progress, development and inventions is birthed. Greatness is good!

Here's How to Become Great...

When I was young, I wanted to be great, but I had a problem. I had the church telling me I should not desire it. I had my white foreign teacher telling me I do not deserve to be great. Then I had parents who said, "Well, try your best to survive." I had my environment and the poverty reinforcing the fact that greatness was out of reach. I had all of this around me, and here comes this guy Jesus telling me, "Anyone can be great."
I was taught, "Don't desire greatness, don't try to be great."

"Look, if you want to be great...," Jesus says. "Look, he that will be great..." Christ says, "Look, I'm going to *show* you how to become great. I know it's natural. Here's the process. You become great by serving yourself to the world."

Matthew 20:26–27
26 Not so with you. Instead, **whoever wants to become great** *[emphasis added] among you must be your servant,*
27 and whoever wants to be first must be your slave.

When Jesus spoke to His leadership trainees, a.k.a. disciples, about this, He did not tell them that it was wrong to want to be great. He acknowledged that it is natural to want greatness, and He told them how to achieve it. He did not discourage the desire for greatness. That may shock you, because that is the opposite of your image of Jesus. Everything we think about Him is the opposite of that, that He was a humble, nice fellow who wanted everyone to be a doormat—turn the other cheek and so on. Most of us were taught that this man Jesus said to be humble, be kind to everybody, and not desire to be great. We were taught to be subservient as the mark of humility and therefore of spiritual greatness.

Jesus said *whosoever will be great.* That means the guy under the bridge or the guy sleeping in the castle. He places greatness in the grasp of every human. This takes leadership out of the hand of the elite few, the privileged few, and into the hand of any human who learns the secret.

He is saying that greatness is not only possible but also accessible; and it is accessible to every human — *whoever*.

Here He is, in essence, saying, "Hey, guys, you want to be great? I've got the secret." If you want to become great in My kingdom, you don't own people. You don't control people. You don't manipulate people. You don't oppress people. You don't threaten people. You don't use people in My system. Leadership in My kingdom, My country, is serving yourself to the people."

"Not so with you. Instead, whoever wants to become great among you must be your **servant,** *and whoever wants to be first must be your* **slave"** (*Matthew 20:26–27*, emphasis added). He meant this: whoever wants to be the first one people look for when they want something done has to be the *slave of his gift.*

If you want to be great, the greatest will be the one who is the servant of all. He serves everyone what he has. What does he have? He has his gift. If you refine your gift, develop your gift and then serve your gift to the world, you become great.

You can read the great thinkers on management, business, and philosophy, from the philosopher Plato to the organizational management expert Peter Drucker, and you will not find in any other book the idea expressed in this lesson. Even in Christ's additional sessions on leadership with His disciples, it is the same idea (*Matthew 20:26, Matthew 23:11, Mark 10:43, Luke 22:26*).

We can isolate Jesus as a philosopher, not as the Son of God, to test how His leadership theories stack up against others and to observe how He modeled it in His own life. When we do, His idea outshines all the other theories. That idea is that leadership has nothing to do with ruling people. It has more to do with your gift — identifying it, maximizing it, and serving that gift to the world.

Defying Conventional Thinking

The concept of leadership Jesus introduced is so radical that it demands a **paradigm shift from the idea that followers serve leaders to the idea that leaders serve the world.** His philosophy of leadership

defies the contemporary leadership status quo. By conventional thinking, the concept of greatness, or leadership, is: "How many people do
you control? If you are a leader, how many people work under you?
How many people look to you, how many people worship you? How
many people admire you? How many are afraid of you? How many
'direct reports' do you have? How many people are on your payroll?
How many people do you influence?" All these are the old concepts of
greatness.

The philosophy of Jesus turns these concepts on their heads. The
concept of greatness from the world is, "How many people serve you?"
He reverses it: "How many people do you serve?" He bases His idea of
leadership on completely different values. You cannot measure true
leadership by how many people serve you, but by how many people
you serve. He says, in essence, and I paraphrase this, "[I] did not come to
be served, but to serve myself to the world."

Matthew 20:28
Just as the Son of Man did not come to be served, but to serve, and to give his life as
a ransom for many.

Baby of the Family

Jesus shifts the balance. He says, "I am introducing a new leadership
philosophy today. The greatest among you shall be *the youngest*."

Luke 22:26
But you are not to be like that. Instead, the greatest among you should be like the
youngest, and the one who rules like the one who serves.

Remember before, He said "servant." In this seminar for the disciples,
He shifts it. He changes the word. He uses the phrase "the youngest."

Let me tell you my experience as the youngest. I am from a family of eleven children in which I am number six. For a time, I was the youngest—with five older siblings. The youngest is the one who all the other five call on to do everything. "Go get my shoes." "Bring me a glass of water." "Turn the TV off." "Bring that paper here." "Bring me that book." "Shut up." "Go over there." "Clean that." "Get out of here."

The youngest is the one who does everything. They call on him to do everything.

It is amazing to me that I serve my elder brothers and sisters even today. They are members of my organization. The majority of our family is serving in leadership positions somewhere in our community today. I think it is because of how we have seen the model of leadership from our parents. My eldest brother, Oscar, would go out of his way to help people, give his money away, and use his service to help other people. He is a contractor and a builder who sometimes helps other people build their homes and turns it over to them as a gift. I want to say, "What are you doing?" but I think that is leadership.

My elder sister, Sheila, is my administrative assistant. She constantly wants to help other people become better. All of my elder sisters have worked all their lives as public servants, in leadership positions. My whole family has served the community in some area of significance. The influence of servant leadership has always been with me.

The First Person They Call

The Bible says you are great when they keep calling on you. You are great when you develop your gift so well that the first person they think of when they want something done is you. Do not consider that abuse. That is greatness. The other people are not producing; you are.

That is why the busy are busy. You know the old saying, "If you want something done, give it to a busy person"? They already know how to get things done. Most of those who are not busy are not looking for anything to do. If you give them something to do, they will not get it done.

The greatest among you shall be like the youngest, the child who has to do everyone else's bidding. "Why me again?" "Because you are great!" "Pick on somebody else!" "No, you are great. I can trust you. You get things done."

Jesus says, basically, "If you want to be the greatest, be like the youngest, and the one who rules will be like the one who serves." He says, "Look. You want to be the one ruling everything? The way you get into a ruling position is to be the one who seems to be serving all the time."

If the company you work for avoids calling on you, you have a problem. The word *done* means "execute," taken from the word *executive*. An executive gets things done. If they do not call on you, that is a bad sign.

When a company like Disney or AT&T begins to lose money, they do not fire the workers; they fire the CEO. The chief executive officer. Why? He just is not getting things done.

God hates laziness. God loves volunteers. People who run from responsibility will never have it. Do not wait for them to call on you. "I will clean the bathroom, I will clean it. I! Me, me!"

When you hide from responsibility, God hides greatness from you. When you make yourself valuable, people look for you. If they do not miss you, you are in trouble. You are a nuisance. Greatness is evident when they miss you. You rule so much when you are around that they miss you when you are absent. Your gift is so valuable, people send for you.

Scripture says a person's gift opens the way and brings him into the presence of the great.

Proverbs 18:16
A gift opens the way for the giver and ushers him into the presence of the great.

I have been in meetings with heads of state, heads of corporations and heads of churches. I sit in these meetings with these great leaders who want my advice, and I think, "What am I doing here? How did I get here? Why is this man asking me these questions?" These questions affect the whole country, and I am thinking: "They called for my gift. They don't know me personally, but they know my gift." Top-level companies and governments sometimes call on me because of my gift.

It humbles me, and it recalls the story of Joseph of the Old Testament. Joseph had a gift. He had a reputation for interpreting dreams, but he was in prison.

Genesis 41:14–15
14 So Pharaoh sent for Joseph, and he was quickly brought from the dungeon. When he had shaved and changed his clothes, he came before Pharaoh.
15 Pharaoh said to Joseph, "I had a dream, and no one can interpret it. But I have heard it said of you that when you hear a dream you can interpret it."

When the king needed that gift, he sent for Joseph. It does not matter where people are. If word gets out about their gift, they are the first ones people think about, and people in need of the gift call for them. A gift brought Joseph before great men. It brought him before the great leader of Egypt. Joseph was not important. His gift was.

People will never make you great. Your gift will make you great. The more efficiently you serve that gift to the world, the greater you become to the world.

Leaders for Today

Since Jesus, no one—no philosopher, no professor, no ideology—has ever introduced anything to improve on His idea that we exist to serve humanity, not to be served by it. Every college in our contemporary world needs a special course on servant leadership. Our contemporary world leaders need to be reintroduced to the idea of Jesus and to His idea of leadership. We keep producing corporate leaders whose goal is to serve their own coffers, rather than to serve the community.

If companies want to succeed, they should strive not to be great companies but to be serving companies. Maybe presidents of companies and CEOs should ask different questions—not, how much money can we get from a customer, but how much better can we serve the customer? How can we make customers' lives easier and more convenient?

How can we give them better quality? If the organizations of the world strive to become servant leaders, they will become great companies and entities in their generation.

I believe that the demise of any organization is when individuals who are more concerned about the organization than they are about the market that they serve become the heads of it. The corporate leaders become so interested in their personal perquisites and their personal salaries that they lose the very purpose on which they founded the company, which was to provide an improvement or pleasure for the customer.

The twenty-first century is still in desperate need of the first-century idea that Jesus introduced in servant leadership. Defective leadership always attempts to use authority to control people. Defective leaders exercise authority over people and "call themselves Benefactors."

Luke 22:25
Jesus said to them, "The kings of the Gentiles Lord it over them; and those who exercise authority over them call themselves Benefactors."

Benefactors is a telling word. These rulers Lorded it over the people but claimed their motivation was really to help them. They said they were just being benevolent, doing good things for them. They used people for their own purposes and pretended it was for the people's benefit.

The traditional paradigm is that leaders benefit from followers: "Use them to benefit yourself. Tax them without representation. Take the biggest portion of their crop and keep them in debt to you. Keep wages low and maximize profit. Discriminate against and harass the female aides. Require overtime but provide no benefits. Play hardball in the labor negotiations. Give the contract to the one who will pay you a kickback."

This is not leadership. Yet this describes much leadership in the world today. Using the people to benefit the rulers. Feeding off people's fears to intimidate them. Threatening people to maintain control.

How Would Jesus Lead?

Jesus was born as a member of a colony of the Roman Empire. He was born as a subject of an imperial power, and the solution He gave to oppression by the most powerful imperial government in history was servant leadership. His answer to the problem was that we can just serve, rather than be served. He used the Roman Empire as an example of what happens to society when government does not serve the people. He said to reverse that because good government is focused on serving the people, rather than being served.

If Jesus Christ came back to earth today, I believe His first reaction would be to disassociate Himself with 90 percent of the people who claim they represent Him. He would rebuke every other system that is controlling, pressing, manipulating, or ruling humanity. If you consider the world two thousand years ago, the situation is not much different today. Instead of one empire, we have multiple empires, but their policies have the same results.

Jesus would probably say that the rulers of this world love to Lord over the people, love to exact tribute from the people, instead of serving, but it will not be so with *you*—this new generation of servant leaders in the making. He might ask, "What government today has the genuine interest of the people at heart? What corporation? What school? What church?"

It will not be so with you.

Understanding the Principles

The words *servant* and *leader* together would seem to be a paradox, an oxymoron, but the term fits the concept of Jesus. I have studied it and distilled it into seven principles for audiences all over the world. The principles are these:

Leadership Is...

1. **Leadership is *predetermined, not preference.*** Leadership is not something you do; it is something you are. You cannot retire from it, as a bird cannot retire from flight. Just before Jesus laid

out His idea that you had to be a servant, a mere slave even, to be great, the disciples were arguing about position, wanting preferred slots. "We prefer to sit there," they said. He said, "Look, you can't prefer in God's kingdom. It's already predetermined."

Matthew 20:23
Jesus said to them, "You will indeed drink from my cup, but to sit at my right or left is not for me to grant. These places belong to those for whom they have been prepared by my Father."

There is a place in God's Kingdom administration for you and every other human on earth. No one can take your unique spot of gifting, and you cannot take anyone else's spot either. These places—these positions of authority, greatness, and leadership—belong to each one of us specifically designed, preselected and fashioned for that particular spot of gifting. The Creator is preparing you for what he has prepared for you. Your position of leadership preceded your conception. You were built with spiritual, mental and physical circuitry for your specific leadership gift.

2. **Leadership is *a prepared position*.** In God's kingdom, everybody has a place set aside. It is a leadership position, and it is prepared for you. God predesigned your spot before he made you. He made you to fit the spot. "You don't go looking for it," Jesus says. "The Father has already prepared it. He has set aside places for everyone who is supposed to have them" (see *Matthew 20:23*). When you prepare something, it means you establish it beforehand. What you were born to do is, in effect, predestined. You can refuse to fulfill it, but you will suffer bitterly as you turn into something God did not intend.

3. **Leadership *demands a price*.** To get to your spot, you have to pay a price. Jesus said, "You have to drink the cup to sit in your spot." *Matthew 20:22 "You don't know what you are asking," Jesus said to them. "Can you drink the cup I am going to drink?" "We can," they answered.* Even though you were born to be a leader in your arena, it comes at a price. It is a process of preparation, training, development,

and refinement. The position is prepared for you, but you have to prepare yourself for that position.

4. **Leadership is *inherent*.** Leadership is not given to you by request or by prayer. You are born with it. Whether you develop it, whether you use it, whether you actualize it, whether you deploy it, is totally up to you, but the capacity is built in. Few of us will ever need to drive our car ninety miles an hour, but the capability is there. The manufacturer put it there. Humanity is the only part of creation that has this choice, this problem of whether to use our capabilities. God built in this unique component called the will. We *can* decide to not be what we are supposed to be.

5. **Leadership is *a divine deposit*.** When Jesus told his colleagues James and John that their Father had already "secured a place for you" (*John 14:3*), He was implying that they were requesting someone else's position, and they were appealing to Him to get it for them. It was not His decision, not His to give, but the decision had been made and the security deposit had been paid. We do not get to decide what our leadership gift is. It is deposited in our very being. He says to us, "Look, God has arranged this, and I cannot give you anyone else's position. You can fast and pray, but I can't change the positions."

6. **Leadership is *not for you, but for others*.** What you were born to do is serve. Your gift is not for you. It is there so you can serve it to others. Leadership is like a smile. When you smile, others can see it, but you cannot. It benefits others more than it does you. The car does not exist just to get itself from place to place. It exists to transport someone. Leadership is service.

7. **Leadership is *becoming yourself for the benefit of others*.** Become yourself. Leadership is not something you do; it is something you *become*. You have to find out what you were born to become. That is your area of domain. Becoming yourself is a process that begins with self-discovery. If you are ready to take the journey, ask yourself:

Who am I?
What is my gift?
How and whom can I serve?

PART 2

THE SEVEN PRINCIPLES OF SERVANT LEADERSHIP

5

This Is My Spot: Go Find Yours

PRINCIPLE 1
PREDETERMINED AND NOT A PREFERENCE

"There is room for everyone at the top."

G overnment leaders wanted to build a highway that would come right through a little town. In the highway's path was a Buddhist temple, a most sacred place. The government spent so much money on the highway that it could not change the routing of it, so the authorities decided to relocate the temple to a beautiful place on a hill.

They brought in archaeologists, architects, other specialists, and workers, and they began to dismantle this temple, stone by stone, so they could later replicate the original. In the middle of the old temple was its most precious object—a huge statue of Buddha. The people had come there to worship every day for centuries.

The workers brought in a crane to lift the Buddha. They put the big fastening chains around it and prayed, "Don't let anything happen to this Buddha"; for they, too, had come here most of their lives to worship before this massive clay Buddha. As they lifted the Buddha above the ground, suddenly the arm fell off. Everybody began to weep, and then the other arm broke, and then the ear fell off, and it was too late to stop. By the time they moved it over to the new location, most of the clay had fallen away.

The workers were so depressed, and the government was afraid the people would rebel against it. The whole village stood around the Buddha as the clay continued to fall to the ground. Suddenly, the people saw something they never knew existed—there appeared under all that clay a pure gold Buddha statue. Their ancestors had hidden it under clay so thieves would not steal the pure gold one.

The Buddha could not shine until somebody moved it. It had been in the wrong spot.

Leaders are born when people discover their gift and find their place. They must first discover what is inside, underneath the clay. In the same way, leaders have to discover what is inside them to connect with their spot. When you connect with your spot, your gift comes alive.

When you feel your arm fall off as you continue to read about servant leadership, do not panic. When you feel the identity that you love so much come apart, let it go. When your old concepts begin to crack, let them.

Every human has a place in the universe of humanity. The universe has a place for your gift. Nevertheless, if you are like the average person, you probably have lived most of your life in a job that is not right for you, placing you in constant stress and conflict with who you are.

Each of us must find our spot. Only you can occupy your spot, and no one need be jealous of anyone else's spot. Our spot is the place we are supposed to be, being who we simply *are* by nature.

When we are not ourselves, we experience stress. When we are not where we should be—physically, emotionally, spiritually—we experience stress. The Creator did not build humans to live with stress, and much of the stress we experience results from being in the wrong spot. Most human illness and disease is a result of stress, the "fight or flight" hormones that get out of control.

The hormone adrenaline exists to give us bursts of energy that we need temporarily to cope with danger—to run from a lion or engage in hand-to-hand combat with the invading tribe, for instance. We have all heard stories of petite mothers lifting cars off babies in the heat of crisis—a feat attributed to adrenaline.

Danger is usually a short-term situation, but when a situation is chronic—wrong job, wrong marriage, wrong habit—the body becomes stuck in crisis mode. It keeps pumping up the adrenaline over the long haul, like gunning the accelerator and keeping the brake on. Even a pleasurable activity that the body reads as stress—driving a race car or playing computer games—can pump up our adrenaline. Some people seem to seek out stress, drama, and constant crisis to maintain the rush, for the thrill of it. Whatever the cause, the body, mind, and emotions do not handle long-term stress well. This eventually takes its toll on the heart and other systems of the body.

Many people become stuck in this stress mode. Unhappy with their jobs, they produce adrenaline because stress activates their "flight" instinct. Maybe they need the money and feel they have to stay on the job, living every day under stress. Conflict with the boss may trigger the body to "fight"—even when the mind knows that is out of the question in the civilized setting of the workplace—in the corporate boardroom, or during labor negotiations.

These frustrated workers cannot wait to get home, because for them home is like freedom from prison—the prison of stress. You want to leave your job, but you have to stay there because of a thing called salary. That means you live your whole day under stress.

Or maybe your situation is just the opposite. You love your work and practically live at the office to escape a bad home environment. You work long hours to avoid a nagging spouse or bad children or overbearing parents.

By the word *spot*, I mean your place in the universe of humanity. About 6.7 billion people live in the world today, and God has designed a spot for each of us, including one just for you. The average person dies never finding that spot, doing something they were not born to do. This is why their lives are miserable and why they are frustrated.

Stress is pressure placed on your life—your body, your soul, and your spirit—that you were not designed to handle. Premature death is a product of people being out of their spot in life, because stress kills.

In My Father's House

The opposite of stress is peace. Peace. Imagine earning pay for being at peace. Imagine leaving home every day to enter peace. Peace all the time was God's original plan for you. That is why we call Him the Prince of Peace (see *Isaiah 9:6*). He is the God of peace. He is not a god of stress.

My goal is to help you find a home. You were born to stay home. I am not talking about a house. Home is similar to when people in sports refer to being "in the zone." "Boy, Tiger is really in the zone today." He is home, in his spot, his mansion.

When Jesus was preparing His aides for His departure, they brought up the issue of greatness again. Everybody was jockeying for position, but He more or less said, "Why are you worrying? I do not want you to panic. There's a mansion for everybody."

John 14:1–2 kjv
1 Let not your heart be troubled: ye believe in God, believe also in me.
2 In my Father's house are many mansions: if it were not so, I would have told you. I go to prepare a place for you.

The word that is translated *"mansion"* in the King James Version in Hebrew means "place of authority." We have actually distorted that to mean something else, and this has caused many problems. The word *mansion* is a poor translation. The NIV uses the word *rooms*. Then Jesus adds, "I go to prepare a place."

John 14:1–2 niv
1 Do not let your hearts be troubled. Trust in God; trust also in me.
2 In my Father's house are many rooms; if it were not so, I would have told you. I am going there to prepare a place for you.

He used the same word when He told James and John He could not give them the positions they wanted, when He said, "These places belong" (*Matthew 20:23*).

By contemporary definitions, *place* has many meanings, including these:

- *Mansion — estate*
- *Place of authority*
- *Position of power*
- *Place of influence*
- *Authorized position*
- *Home — natural place (Estate)*
- *Position of impact*

When a person is out of their spot—gift, position, strength—life torments them. They are unfulfilled, angry, bitter, confused, frustrated, and sad. They make others around them uncomfortable. When a person is not in their place, their mansion, their home, their position of authority where they have their full gifting, they are frustrated.

But when they are in their spot they are in their zone of destiny and can function at maximum potential. Your leadership spot is like a screw finding its right nut. It is like the last missing piece of a puzzle finding its slot. For me, when I am not speaking to people about leadership, writing about it, or thinking about it, I am under stress. This is *home* for me. My enjoyment of life comes from being in my leadership spot. I would pay to do it. I should pay you for letting me be myself, who I am. I do not have stress in my life because I have found my spot. It is beautiful to find your spot. God has a spot for everyone.

It's Not a Competition

I invite you to get out of the rat race. After all, if you win, you will simply be the big rat. Stop running in the competition. The only person you should compete with in life is yourself. Ask yourself, "How well am I performing in my leadership spot?"

The battery does not compete with a spark plug, because the battery knows the spark plug can never be a battery, and vice versa. They sit in the engine in their spots and serve the engine their gift without competing against each other.

None of the billions of people on earth right now is a substitute for you. The Creator has prepared a place among them just for you. Servant leadership was the only concept of leadership Jesus taught. He believed that every human being possessed leadership potential. The reason you suffer from jealousy is that you think people can take your spot. The reason you are suspicious of everybody is that you are afraid someone can take your place in life. The reason you covet other people's goods is that you believe they can take what belongs to you. The reason you compete with other people for positions in life is that you believe places of advancement and advantage are scarce.

The tendency of people to pull down those in their own group—the poor, minority people, women, other interns, fellow vice presidents—who are trying to get ahead is where the phrase "crabs in a barrel" comes from. If you understand and adopt a servant-leadership mentality, there is no need for that.

When you understand leadership as Jesus taught it, you will never be jealous again. Jealousy is only possible when you believe someone has something that belongs to you. If I understand that you never can have what belongs to me and that I never can have what belongs to you and what belongs to me can only fit me, then I will never envy you.

You can be confident in your gifting and your place in the world. Any success I have can never have a negative effect on you. Likewise, your success cannot have a negative effect on me. It is my prayer that, as you find your spot and explore your area of gifting, you will put aside all your jealousy. All of your competition, all of your fear, and all of your suspicion of other people will be left behind. When you stake a claim on your spot, your gifting, you will never wonder again whether someone can take your spot. You will know that if anybody tries to fit in your spot, the spot will destroy them, because the Creator did not build it for them.

God Prepared Your Spot

James and John were two of Jesus' favorites. James, John, and Peter were the "big three." Yet even as the favorites, they could not get the spots they requested (*Matthew 20:20–23*), because leadership is prepared by God, not by preference. You cannot tell God, "I prefer to be there." Why? He did not prepare you for that spot there and did not prepare that spot there for you. Both are prepared. You belong to "it" and "it" belongs to you. The spot belongs to you, and you belong to the spot.

When you connect with your spot, your gift comes alive—and so do you. When you are not in your place, you have stress and burnout. The burnout is probably a sign that you are in the wrong spot. If you have to struggle, you are out of your spot. If it wears you out, you are out of your spot. Your spot will give you energy, not deplete it.

The shape of the spot has already predetermined your shape, so if anybody attempts to squeeze into your spot, the irritation will kill them. It will wear them out. They will have to struggle and fight to be in that spot. It takes energy and pain that will cause burnout. Why? Your spot does not fit them.

Matthew 20:24
When the ten heard about this, they were indignant with the two brothers.

It causes irritation in the whole organization when you are out of place.

A human out of spot is like a virus. He infects the whole organization. If he is not built for it, he will disrupt the whole organization. This disruption is an infection. A virus is a foreign body. It is not supposed to be there, and it can make the whole body sick.

Sometimes on the job you wonder, "Why is this not working?" It is because the people are in the wrong spots. They irritate you all day. They are always gossiping, angry, frustrated. They irritate others because they are not fitting the position for which you hired them. They are in places prepared for someone else.

If you run an organization, a company, or a home, and you hire people or place your children and spouse in arbitrary positions, based on their credentials or on favoritism—"This one has a degree"; "That one has always been special to me"—not on their gifting, you will see problems. The person in the wrong spot becomes disruptive. The organization becomes dysfunctional. We might have to fire them or reorganize.

To know the right places for people, we must know their areas of gifting. They may not even know it. Leaders recognize the gifts in others. A teacher might discover that the stammering child who can hardly utter a sentence sings like an angel and can direct the Christmas production. The boss who is a true leader discovers that the kid with the dreadlocks working in the mailroom is a genius at designing interactive Web sites and places him in the right spot.

The Wrong Spot

History is full of stories of people who were not in their proper spots. One of the first who comes to mind is Adam. The fall of humankind, as related in the biblical text by Moses, was the road that Adam took. God created Adam to serve Eve. The fall of man came after Eve served Adam. She gave him something, when he should have been the one serving her. He took the fruit from her, and that was the turning of the tables.

Genesis 3:17
To Adam he said, "Because you listened to your wife and ate from the tree about which I commanded you, 'You must not eat of it,' cursed is the ground because of you; through painful toil you will eat of it all the days of your life."

The second one not in his proper spot who comes to mind is Abraham's nephew Lot. God positioned Lot to serve with Abraham, yet Lot decided that he would go off by himself and separate himself from his uncle. Of course, the results were disastrous, and he ended up in an environment where he should not have been. It was destructive for him, and his presence affected the whole city in Sodom.

Genesis 13:11–12
11 So Lot chose for himself the whole plain of the Jordan and set out toward the east. The two men parted company.
12 Abram lived in the land of Canaan, while Lot lived among the cities of the plain and pitched his tents near Sodom.

Jonah was another Bible figure out of his leadership spot. He was given an assignment and decided to go in another direction. He hopped aboard a ship to run away from God's purpose.

Jonah 1:3
But Jonah ran away from the Lord and headed for Tarshish. He went down to Joppa, where he found a ship bound for that port. After paying the fare, he went aboard and sailed for Tarshish to flee from the Lord.

He affected everyone on that ship (see *Jonah 1:5*). That is the issue. When you are out of position, you affect other people. Jonah also affected the whole city of Nineveh; he could have actually caused the disaster or destruction of the whole city by his disobedience. He also personally suffered. Everything around him was wrong: a city could be destroyed, a ship was out in the stormy sea, and a fish swallowed him. This is an example of the power of dislocation, of being out of position.

For a more recent example, consider Hitler. He was a very talented and gifted man in oratory, in persuasive speech, in being able to communicate effectively. As we know, he became preoccupied with the destruction of a group of people, rather than the improvement of a nation, and the results were horrendous. Today we almost hate to call his name. He was out of position. In his right spot he might have improved Germany's lot, not devalued and destroyed a group of people. I do not think the German people wanted to kill six million Jews, but Hitler led them in that direction. Today many Germans are ashamed of that, but the question is, how did they allow that? How did they let someone lead them to devalue human life, to introduce an ideology to justify it?

Any time you devalue people, you are out of position. Servant leadership is about serving the interests of the people and meeting their needs. All of humanity becomes your concern.

What a Deal!

Those who know their leadership spot and understand their gift are the happiest. Your gift is fun. You enjoy it, you can do it all day, and, remember, they pay you to do it.

Somebody asked Tiger Woods, "What is your hobby?"

He said, "Golf."

The interviewer asked, "What do you enjoy?"

"Golf."

"When are you the happiest?" he was asked next.

"When I'm playing golf."

It makes him happy, he looks happy doing it, and companies pay him millions because people enjoy watching him. He is in his spot.

If you were to ask him who he was, he would say, "Man, I am golf and I give my life to this game. I think it, drink it, smell it, smoke it; I sleep it. When I am doing nothing, I am thinking about it."

He gives it for the multitudes. We get the pleasure from seeing him playing it. Tiger Woods is having fun, but we get the pleasure. He gives it to the world.

The beauty of serving your gift is that your wealth is coming from what you enjoy. You enjoy being yourself. Nobody should pass up this deal. This is a perfect deal.

It is like a bird saying, "I am a bird, they pay me to fly. I like flying. They call me great because I can fly. I am the first creature they think of when they want to know about flight. Did you know we birds are leaders in the category of flight?"

A bird gets energy *from* flying. That is how a bird can leave Alaska and fly nonstop to Brazil.

Some people come to my seminars and wonder, "How can he teach for two hours straight and still be excited and energetic?" It is because I am in my spot. You can listen to some people speak, and after ten minutes you have to turn them off because even they seem bored. They are probably supposed to be doing something else.

Leadership is having something for which everybody is going to come to you. They line up for it. Whatever gift you have attracts people—customers, potential employees, new church members, or voters. That is the ultimate principle of servant leadership.

"You don't go looking for it," Jesus essentially says. "The Father has already prepared it."

Matthew 20:23
Jesus said to them, "You will indeed drink from my cup, but to sit at my right or left is not for me to grant. These places belong to those for whom they have been prepared by my Father."

He has prepared a place. Your leadership is in your spot—your area of gifting.

It's My Pleasure

When you are in your leadership spot, work is joy. When you find that spot, going to work is pleasure.

Drew Carey, a popular American stand-up comic, accepted the job to replace Bob Barker when he retired after thirty-five years as host of the television show *The Price Is Right*. Someone asked Carey if he ever needed a break from being funny.

He replied that he hoped he'd never need a break and that he didn't feel there was such a thing as too much fun. He relished his role as someone who helped others feel good.

When the reporter asked Carey why he took the job, he said, he thought giving away prizes didn't really seem like a job to him, but more like a good time.

He told the *New York Times* that the most important factor was that he looked forward to giving away a new car, refrigerator, or vacation to someone who might really need it. He added that, away from the show, he often personally tips people at least $100—even for a hamburger or a cola—and sometimes much more. He enjoyed sharing his own wealth, and was looking forward to doing that on an even larger scale on *The Price Is Right.*

He is in his spot. He can use his gift for the benefit of others.

In a similar fashion, when an American television interviewer asked the comedian and actor D. L. Hughley whether he might be interested in political leadership, he said, "Me, I tell jokes."

Hughley's gift is comedy too. He and Carey earn their money by making other people laugh. People pay them to make them happy for a few minutes. They are leaders in the domain of comedy.

Neither article about Carey suggested, nor did he say, that religious beliefs had anything to do with his motivation to give. The idea of using your gifts to benefit others transcends religion. It works whether one is a student and follower of the rabbi Jesus or not.

R-E-S-P-E-C-T

Leadership has nothing to do with titles either. It has to do with function. I respect you because of your gift, not because of your title. If you have no title at all, once I discover your function and its value to me, I will protect you. I will pay you to give it to me. That is what makes you wealthy. Wealth does not come from your job; it comes from your gift.

Respect is a result of your gift. It does not come because you seek it. Respect is from the manifestation of your function, your gift, your leadership spot. That is why they call on me, and that is why people who need your gift call on you. When you have a dental problem, who do you look for? A dentist. You respect him because he has a function. You will drive twenty minutes to find him, and then give him your money too.

The same thing is true about all of life. Your specialty makes you valuable, and everyone was born with a specialty.

Disrespect is ignorance of function. What about you? Have you shaken off the clay? Are you in the right leadership spot?

6

Who Died and Left You in Charge?: The Dominion Mandate

PRINCIPLE 2

A PREPARED POSITION

"He who would lead others must first become his own follower."

At a recent seminar I conducted, a woman asked: "I wanted to know if you could just make something clear for me. You said that everyone is a leader. If everyone is a leader, but doesn't have dominion over people, what are they leaders over?"

"You were born to dominate an area of gifting, not to dominate people," I told her. "When you dominate your area of gifting, you attract people. So do not focus on the people. Focus on your gift."

- You were created to dominate, but not over people.
- You were created to dominate in your area of gifting.
- Your leadership is in your area of gifting.

Humans, both men and women, were specifically entrusted with, endowed with, dominion over the things of the earth, but not the authority to dominate other human beings.

Dominion means to govern, rule, control, manage, lead, to have authority over, to master. We have government, "rulership," control, management, leadership, authority over the fish, the birds, the cattle, the creeping things. God created you and me to exercise leadership over the earth.

Genesis 1:26
Then God said, "Let us make man in our image, in our likeness, and let them rule over the fish of the sea and the birds of the air, over the livestock, over all the earth, and over all the creatures that move along the ground."

You Are Royalty

Ancient Scriptures describe the origins of leadership. If I were to sum-marize the Bible in one statement, it would be this: it is about a *King*, His *kingdom*, and the *King's children*.

The beginning of the first book of Moses declares that "in the begin-ning" the King created the physical universe. "In the beginning God created the heavens and the earth" (*Genesis 1:1*).

The original purpose of the Creator of the world was to extend His heavenly kingdom on earth. His idea was to transfer His influence from his invisible kingdom to a visible realm that he created. His program for transferring that influence was through the leadership of His children.

When I was growing up, the Bahamas Islands constituted a col-ony of Great Britain under a constitutional monarchy. The queen and her family were royalty. The people of the Bahamas were subjects. In the Creator's kingdom, all the citizens are members of the royal family.

The first book of Moses specifies the purpose for humanity's cre-ation: God states His intention to make humans, male and female, in His own image and likeness to rule the fish, the birds, the livestock, the creatures on the ground—in short, the whole earth.

Genesis 1:26–27
26 Then God said, "Let us make man in our image, in our likeness, and let them rule

over the fish of the sea and the birds of the air, over the livestock, over all the earth, and over all the creatures that move along the ground."
27 So God created man in his own image, in the image of God he created him; male and female he created them.

The word *man* in this scripture is plural. It includes both men and women. Further, the King was not creating just two people, but an entire species. "In His own image" refers to humanity's character or nature. The whole species called *man* embodies the image and likeness of the Creator, the King, with His characteristics, qualities, substance, and essence.

In his poem "The Creation," James Weldon Johnson, one of the great Harlem Renaissance writers, puts it this way:

This Great God,
Like a mammy bending over her baby,
Kneeled down in the dust
Toiling over a lump of clay
Till He shaped it in His own image;

Then into it He blew the breath of life,
And man became a living soul.[1]

The Almighty created humans to be kings. The King created humanity in His image and likeness so man and woman could rule. The first book of Moses emphasizes this sovereign authority and legal right to rule. The Creator told the first man and woman to multiply and "rule" the things of the earth:

Genesis 1:28
God blessed them and said to them, "Be fruitful and increase in number; fill the earth and subdue it. Rule over the fish of the sea and the birds of the air and over every living creature that moves on the ground."

In the King James Version of the Bible, the Hebrew word for "rule" —
radah — translates as "have dominion." The Creator made man, the species, in His own nature and own character so that the humans could
rule, have dominion, or "have kingdom" over the earth. Therefore, the
first thing the Creator and King gave to humanity was a kingdom to
oversee. I define *kingdom* as "the governing authority of a king over a
territory, who impacts it with his will, purpose, and intent." He created
earth to be a kingdom in which the offspring of the King would rule
with His authority, and the children would impact it with their will,
purpose, and intent.

The psalmist wrote, *"The highest heavens belong to the Lord, but the earth he
has given to man" (Psalms 115:16)*. Heaven is the Creator's main territory or
domain. He wanted His children to have an active role in His government, so He created a domain for them. In the human kingdoms we
know the heir to a throne cannot become the monarch until the king
or queen dies. For Prince Charles to be king while Queen Elizabeth is
still alive, he would have to rule over a foreign territory. Prince Charles
becomes king of England only if Queen Elizabeth is no longer alive.
Likewise, the heir to the head of state in Japan becomes emperor only
when the current emperor dies.

Yet the Creator of all things is eternal. He will not die, so there is no
succession to the throne of God. Because He lovingly wants Hs children to share in His rule, He created a brand-new kingdom — the visible, physical world of earth — to give humankind a territory to oversee,
under the King's ultimate rule. The Creator is the King of kings; we are
His offspring on earth.

Humanity has the authority to rule over five main earthly realms:
the fish kingdom, the bird kingdom, the animal (livestock) kingdom,
the plant kingdom, and the reptile kingdom (creatures that move
along the ground). Notice that the Creator gave human beings dominion over the earth and the animals, but not over each other. God
created no human to be dominated by another. The Creator's command to humanity was a corporate command: "Let *them* have
dominion."

Establishing Domain

The Creator intended us to be rulers in charge of our physical environment. This we can summarize in the term *dominion mandate*. Here is how this concept relates to servant leadership:

- God's kingdom is one of servant kings who serve it with their gifts.
- God created you to minister to or serve your gifts to the world, fulfilling His purpose on earth.
- Jesus taught that leadership and greatness come from effectively serving your gift to the world.
- Servant leaders measure true leadership by how many people they serve, not by how many people serve them.
- You will always have what you need if you help other people achieve what they want.
- You rule your domain when you serve your gift.
- You supply the world with your gift and your gift will make room for you in the world.

How does this dominion mandate translate to your servant leadership today? To carry out the mandate, you first have to discover your particular domain on earth that you are to rule.

As a royal offspring of the King, You are expected to use your gift to influence the environment around you, your realm of leadership. Leadership is about manifesting your gift. King Solomon said your gift makes room for you in this world and brings you into the presence of the great. *"A gift opens the way for the giver and ushers him into the presence of the great"* (Proverbs 18:16).

When I discovered this truth, everything changed in my life, because I became free from the control of other people and became free to serve the world. Solomon did not say your education or connections would make room for you. Some people can have a Ph.D., have famous relatives, or win a lottery and still be broke.

Others can start with little or nothing and create a fortune. Bill Gates quit college to start the venture that eventually became Microsoft. Why? He discovered his gift. Steve Jobs, cofounder of Apple computers, quit college after only a semester. Why? He discovered his gift. They discovered gifts they could serve to the world. They developed products the world needed, and they became rich and famous. Their gifts have brought them before kings and queens.

Please understand that I am in favor of education, but education cannot *give* you your gift; it can only help you *refine and develop* it, make you more skillful at executing your gift. School, in itself, will not make you successful. Your gift makes you a success. Your gift makes room for you, and it will bring you before kings.

The Master Plan

You may still be thinking, "If everybody was born to lead, then who's going to follow?"

We see a concept of collective human leadership throughout the Scriptures, not just in the first book of Moses. The Creator's original purpose and plan was a kingdom of *kings* ruling earth. It was for "corporate kingship." His purpose was not an organization *with* a leader, but an organization *of* leaders.

In Exodus, the second book of Moses, the Creator told the Israelites their nation would be a treasure if they obeyed Him and kept His covenant. He said the whole earth belonged to Him, but theirs would be *"a kingdom of priests and a holy nation."*

Exodus 19:5–6
5 "Now if you obey me fully and keep my covenant, then out of all nations you will be my treasured possession. Although the whole earth is mine,
6 you will be for me a kingdom of priests and a holy nation." These are the words you are to speak to the Israelites.

Though the King spoke the words to the Israelites, they were to apply to all peoples of the earth. The Israelites were to be an example to the world of what happens when people follow the Creator's original plan.

Later in the history of Israel, the prophet Daniel recorded the Creator's ongoing plan for His offspring to rule—that the people would have sovereignty and His kingdom would be everlasting:

Daniel 7:27
Then the sovereignty, power and greatness of the kingdoms under the whole heaven will be handed over to the saints, the people of the Most High. His kingdom will be an everlasting kingdom, and all rulers will worship and obey him.

This will be a kingdom of rulers worshiping and governing under the ultimate King.

The origins of humanity suggest five principles for understanding your "prepared position."

1. **Every human being was created to lead and designed for dominion.** You have the capacity and ability to dominate in an area of gifting. The Creator gave you a domain to influence on the earth. God created you for *"dominion."* Dominion is the key to servant leadership. God said, "Let them have rulership, mastery, governorship, authority, control, and leadership over the sea, birds of the air, the cattle of the field, and all the earth and everything that creeps upon the ground." He says *"over all the earth"* (*Genesis 1:26*).

2. **Trapped in every follower is a hidden leader.** Everyone who thinks he or she is merely a follower is really a leader trapped in the mind-set of a follower. You do not know who you are. Your enemies may not know who you are either, but they may suddenly want to be your friend when you discover your leadership.

   They do not know you, because you do not know yourself. Your employer pays you a little salary and gives you a little title, and you are proud of that. What a tragedy. You are worth more to the world than anyone could ever pay you. I am convinced that every human in the world was born to solve some problem. You are carrying something that your generation needs. How can you know who you are? Your Creator will introduce you to yourself. He already knows you, even though you or other people do not.

3. **Every human being possesses leadership potential.** All these principles are progressive. Since there is a leader trapped inside every follower, then every human being possesses leadership potential—including you. In the traditional way of thinking, every time you think of leadership, you think of certain elite people. "Servant leadership" says leadership has to do with gifts, and everyone has gifts. Giftedness is not confined to a finite number of people.

4. **Leadership is not only your history but also your destiny.** "Dominion mandate" is not an abstract idea about the origins of humanity. It is just as true today as it was in the beginning. It is what you were meant to do. Every human has a place for his or her gift in the universe of humanity. There is a place for *your* gift. If you find your gift, you will find your place. If you find your place, you will find your leadership.

5. **Though every person was born to lead, each must take action to become a leader.** Every human being must cultivate the spirit of leadership. Just because you were born to be a leader does not mean you will become one. When you discover your place and gift and serve it to the world, the leader within you is born.

A Built-In Capacity

When we think of the word *leadership*, we think of leading people, mastering people, dominating people, or controlling people. Most people who say that they are leaders are really controllers. They try to control people. According to God, humans are off limits to control.

What does God mean when he says man is to dominate? God has given humanity dominion, and whatever God calls for, he provides for. That means whatever God created he designed with the capability to do its job and serve its purpose. If God created birds to fly, then he designed the birds with flight capability on the inside. Whatever God calls for He provides for. When God said let Me make a creature that will have dominion—leadership, rulership, power, control, mastery—He had to create you out of His own material.

If we want a creature that can do all of those things, one who possesses the spirit of dominion and power and authority and mastery and rulership and governorship, we have to build it that way. When the car designers want a model that will run longer and faster on less fuel or a combination of fuels, they have to design it that way and build it to certain specifications.

Birds do not *become* fliers; they *are* fliers. They are born with the capacity. They just have to wait to come of age. When the time is right and their wings are strong enough, the mother will push them out of the nest, and they will know what to do. Likewise, fish do not *become* swimmers; they are born to swim. The ability to float and maneuver in the water is in them.

Humans do not become rulers or leaders. They are born with the capability. They just wait for a season. Everything has its season. Every purpose has its time. "There is a time for everything, and a season for every activity under heaven" (*Ecclesiastes 3:1*).

Trapped in you right now is a hidden leader. You live in a trap set by your environment, by your conditions, by people's opinions, by a culture, by all kinds of traditions, but leadership is built into you.

"Created He Them"

God created humans, male and female. And both received the assignment of dominion over fish and birds and cattle and trees and creeping things. God commissioned both male and female equally to be rulers, governors, leaders, managers, and masters of the earth.

Genesis 1:27–28 kjv
27 So God created man in his own image, in the image of God created he him; male and female created he them.

28 And God blessed them, and God said unto them, Be fruitful, and multiply, and replenish the earth, and subdue it: and have dominion over the fish of the sea, and over the fowl of the air, and over every living thing that moveth.

Yet we see men treating women unequal, at best, and at worst like animals. Most cultures have also oppressed women in some way and cast them in a less-than-equal role. Governments have created laws that burdened them. Churches have denied them positions of author-ity. Corporations have discriminated against them. Schools have often denied them opportunities or educated them to be subservient. Even their own families have sometimes held them back from their dreams.

These things are the opposite of what the Bible teaches. The Word of God explains that God created both man and woman and gave them dominion.

The word *man* is the name God gave to His species. In the biblical account of Adam's line, when God created man, it says he made him in the likeness of God. It says He created the male and female, then blessed them and called *them* "man."

Genesis 5:1–2 kjv
1 This is the book of the generations of Adam. In the day that God created man, in the likeness of God made he him;
2 Male and female created he them; and blessed them, and <u>called their name Adam,</u> (emphasis added) *in the day when they were created.*

"Man" is the name of the species. Therefore, my wife is a "man." Inside of my wife is a "man"—a spirit that is the same image as mine, same value, same ability, same dominion.

1 Peter 3:7
Husbands, in the same way be considerate as you live with your wives, and treat them with respect as the weaker partner and as heirs with you of the gracious gift of life, so that nothing will hinder your prayers.

God created them, male and female, and blessed them. He told both of them to have dominion. This is God's purpose and plan. Thus, every woman is a powerful leader, and every man is a powerful leader as well. Male and female are both leaders with the same ability. You cannot treat a woman as less than a man in value. God blessed them and told them to have dominion *together* over the earth.

If a man can dominate a woman, it would suggest that she is not the image of God. She must be a bird or fish or snake. No, God said He made her in His image and gave her dominion along with her partner. She is the image of God, manifested in the beautiful female body. The Bible also says that in the body of Christ, there is neither male nor female.

Galatians 3:28
"There is neither Jew nor Greek, slave nor free, male nor female, for you are all one in Christ Jesus."

Each must serve the kingdom their gifts, and each is a leader. I do not understand the problem some people have comprehending the woman's role. In our church, my wife, Ruth, is co-pastor, a role many ministers' wives play without the formal recognition. I rarely begin a lecture without declaring my love for her. The PowerPoint for my talks begins with a picture of her and our two children, Charissa and Chairo, with me. In our church, in our home, and in my heart, Ruth has dominion.

7

Jockeying for Position:
The Sons of Zebedee

"Never follow and live for what a man is not willing to die for."

O ne of the greatest lessons I learned in life is never aspire to attain or be jealous of another person's position or achievement in life until I know the price that person paid to get there.

All true success demands a cost, and all great leaders have a story! The price of greatness is the greatness of the price.

Have you ever seen a flashy, new car you really wanted, but realized you would have to make do with your old, beat-up van because the sticker price of the new one was out of your price range?

Leadership also comes at a cost. Many people aspire to it, but not all will pay the price to obtain it. If you do, many want to take your position or at least to be your deputies or in your Cabinet, entourage, or posse, but they may not know or be willing to pay the price you paid. If you are the president of the bank, quarterback of the team, or head of sales, many line up to take your place, but they do not know what you went through to get there. They do not know about the hassles you had and the depression you endured along the way. They do not know you might have had to sell your car or sleep in it, or remortgage your house, to pay for training or supplies. They do not know what it cost you to get through graduate school and how much you still pay in student loans. No one knows how many hours you had to practice and how many injuries you suffered. None of those who covet your position realize how many months you did not earn enough commission to feed your family. Who knows about the discrimination and discouragement you suffered as a woman to get there? Do any of those folks know about the handicap you concealed to avoid obstacles or pity?

Leaders are known not by the medals on their chests but by the scars on their backs.

People might envy Stephen Wynn, for example, a billionaire casino developer who is one of the richest people in America. Do they know he had to take on his family's bingo business before his college graduation when his father suddenly died? Do they realize Wynn has a degenerative eye disease that severely limits his sight? Did they hear on the news that because of his wealth, his daughter was once kidnapped? Would they want to suffer the things he did to get where he is today? Many people might like to be a leader in the gambling world and enjoy his riches, but they would not want his burdens.

A Mother's Plea

The question is never about the position you hold or to which you aspire; it is about the cost.

Remember those two students in the leadership training class of Jesus Christ—James and John, Zebedee's sons? Their desire to become leaders and attain positions of influence and greatness among their peers was conveyed by their mother to their Master-Teacher, Jesus Christ, in this statement:

"Grant that one of these two sons of mine will sit on Your right and the other on Your left in Your kingdom...Look, I want my sons to be Your vice presidents" (*Matthew 20:21*).

Jesus more or less responded: "You don't know what you are asking.

Number one: Can you drink the cup that I am going to drink?" (see *Matthew 20:22*).

The word *cup* here is not literal. It is a Hebrew idiom, a symbol for price or cost. Jesus used this word again in the Garden of Gethsemane:

Matthew 26:39
Going a little farther, he fell with his face to the ground and prayed, "My Father, if it is possible, may this cup be taken from me. Yet not as I will, but as you will."

As the story in Matthew 20 goes, the mother of Zebedee's sons came to this great master and philosopher Jesus Christ asking that her two sons have preferred positions of leadership in his organization. The question is: why did she go to Him? It could be that her sons sent her. Scripture does not say that they sent her, but it says she came.

Matthew 20:20
Then the mother of Zebedee's sons came to Jesus with her sons and, kneeling down, asked a favor of him.

They might have told their mother: "You talk to Jesus for us, and tell him that you would like for your two sons to have the top positions when He establishes His kingdom."

Is this a woman motivated by motherly love, looking out for her kids, as your mother would look out for you? Or are the sons so embarrassed or so secretive that they want advantage over the other ten that they hide behind their mother? Or are they playing to the emotions of the Master, thinking, "Oh, He listens to a woman more than He listens to us. Oh, we will be in trouble because the other guys will be angry. If they get mad, we'll say, 'It was not we who asked. It was our mother.'"

Maybe her husband told her to petition Jesus on behalf of their sons. Perhaps she did it on her own. Parents desire greatness for their children. Zebedee's wife wanted her sons to be great. Parents want their kids to be great even if they do not have money and cannot afford to help them. They do anything to usher their children to greatness — nag the teacher if they feel their child is being held back, pressure the coach to put Sonny in a game, spend their life's savings on their children's education. It is why people in poor countries risk so much to immigrate to wealthier nations, even if they must do it illegally and expose themselves to danger.

Most parents today would admit, "Boy, that's true, I want my kids to be great. I want my kids to make it."

Jesus is saying, "Your kids can make it. And you don't need to have an Ivy League education for your kids to make it; and they don't need that either. They need to discover their gift."

So, here was a mother being a typical parent who wanted her kids to be great. "I want my two boys — when You come into power, when you establish your domain — I want one to be on Your left, one on Your right. Make an offer to my boys. Forget the other ten. Let their parents take care of them. Take care of my boys."

The desire for greatness is normal. The common way people attempt to achieve it is to try to beat the system. The sons of Zebedee, James and John, were trying to beat the system, lining up all their ducks in a row, making sure there is a place for them when Jesus takes command.

This is a normal human experience, but Jesus exposes it.

Jesus responded to her in an interesting way. He was tender with her, very tender. His answer was, "Do you know what you are asking?" His question is loaded. It could have multiple meanings:

1. You do not know what you are saying.
2. What you are asking for is not fair to the others.
3. What you are asking for, I really cannot give you.

All of these could be a part of the answer, but the third one is more likely the principal one.

The Bible says He turned to the sons, which implies that they were probably standing behind Him or aside, letting their mother do the talking, and asked, "Can you drink of the cup that I drink?"

Matthew 20:23
Jesus said to them, "You will indeed drink from my cup, but to sit at my right or left is not for me to grant. These places belong to those for whom they have been prepared by my Father."

That idiom—sacrifice and cost.

His response to them was, "First of all, what you are asking—you don't understand that you don't get it this way. The way you are trying to do this is not the way you are supposed to go about it. I know people do it this way. I understand the system. I can accept the fact that you are trying to do it, but this is not going to work. It never works."

Continuing to explain, He, in effect said, "First of all, let's start off with the question of cost. I didn't get where I am, because I preferred to be here. I got where I am, because I paid a price."

When the other ten heard what James and John asked, Jesus had to deal with discord among His own staff. They were angry, arguing about who was the greatest. They were jockeying for position—trying to get into other people's spots. His response? Ultimately, that whoever wanted to be great must first be a servant, a slave even (see *Matthew 20:27*).

In explaining this to His associates, He did not use the Greek word for *servitude, diakonos*. He used the word that means "to give yourself out." The word in Greek is *doulos*, meaning "slave, bond, voluntary servant."

Prepared for Greatness

Leadership requires preparation, and the preparation is part of the cost. You have to prepare yourself for that which is prepared for you. If you look at leaders in history, they had to go through a process to accomplish greatness. Abraham Lincoln, Martin Luther King Jr., and Mahatma

Gandhi were born for greatness, but each had to pay a price. Like the princes and princesses who will grow up in the king's household and will inherit the kingdom, they had to be trained for leadership. Ultimately, each of them paid with their lives; each was assassinated for their causes.

The New York real-estate tycoon Donald Trump has children who would no doubt inherit a great deal of money if they had never studied or worked a day in their lives, but like him, they have gone to the finest business schools. They are working their way up in his operation to prepare for greatness, just as he worked in his father's real-estate business. His television program *The Apprentice*, has been wildly popular in the United States, perhaps because people are fascinated by how one prepares for greatness. Each season's winner has paid a price in time, sweat, and tears to make it.

Likewise, when the sons of the publishers of newspapers like the *Washington Post* or the *New York Times* succeed them, the general reader thinks, "Of course, he gave it to his own flesh and blood." What they do not see is that often those heirs have worked at the paper—or one owned by someone else—every day for years, maybe decades, paying dues and learning the workings of the company, from delivering papers to reporting news to selling ads. They paid a price.

For you to get to your leadership spot, you, too, have to prepare and pay a price, as Jesus taught. It is going to cost you. Just settle down, get ready to pay the price. No one will hand it to you.

God does not establish the price; it is set by your environment. When you find what you were born to do, your enemies come alive. When you are not in your leadership spot, people may like you because you are just like them—lost. However, when you find out who you really are and decide to go for it, all hell will break loose on you. Even in your own house, your enemies can rise. When you find your true self, others may hate you, because now they cannot make you who they want you to be anymore. When you discover your real self, they cannot manipulate you anymore.

People hate it when they cannot control you. Friends may turn on you. Your own family may turn on you. The company may decide, "This is just not the right fit. We are going to have to let you go." You might even be put out of your church or your condo building.

You can always tell when you are getting close to your leadership spot, because people suddenly begin to say, "Who do you think you are?"

Let me assure you, however, it is worth the price. You are going to find that place, and you are going to set people free.

When You Ask the Wrong Question

Jesus was concerned about the fact that His leadership students desired to pursue greatness by the same process taught in their culture, and the culture of the Romans, which is where we get our leadership philosophy. He was correcting that, when He began by saying, "If you want to be great, you have to ask the right question." The question that the mother of James and John should have asked was, "What is the price to sit on Your right and left? What is the cost? What would they have to do to earn it, Lord?"

As you recall, she had asked that her two sons have the top positions in the company—"in your kingdom." A kingdom is the governing influence of a king over a territory. It is a government, not a religion.

Imagine the conversation:

The mother: "Look, I want my sons to be your vice presidents."
Jesus: "You don't know what you are asking. Number one, can you drink the cup that I am going to drink? Can you really make these sacrifices to be leaders?"
James and John: "Oh, Yes, Jesus! We can! We can!"
Jesus: "You will drink from it all right, but I can't do anything for you. Those jobs are not mine to hand out."

It is amazing how quickly we can respond when power is at stake. When Jesus used the word *cup* again in the Garden of Gethsemane, he was praying and struggling with the price He had to pay for humanity (see *Matthew 26:39*). Here James and John are asking for positions of leadership and power. He connects the position with a cup. He said,

"Every position has a price." That means you do not ask for positions. Wrong question. You ask, "What is the cost to sit there?"

The question is never about the position; it is about the price.

"What does it cost, Dr. Munroe, to be on television all over the world?" Sit down for two days and let me tell you, because that's how long it will take to introduce what I went through. After the first hour, you will say, "Forget being on TV around the world. I'm going back to driving a van."

It is easy to criticize Oral Roberts—evangelist, healer, and founder of the university I attended. Easy! You do not know the cup.

Titles do not make leaders; cups make leaders.

To James and John, Jesus said, "Can you drink the cup?" and He was thinking, "They want to sit on My level."

He said, "Oh, you want to sit on My level? Then you have to drink the cup. You have to pay the same price that I paid to sit here."

They said, "We can."

Now watch his response: "You will indeed drink"—watch this word—"from My cup."

He did not say, "You will drink my cup."

His cup is crucifixion. If you study history, you will find that both James and John died horrific deaths. Scripture says James was executed by sword, and tradition holds that John was exiled and later boiled in hot oil.

Acts 12:1–2
1 It was about this time that King Herod arrested some who belonged to the church, intending to persecute them.
2 He had James, the brother of John, put to death with the sword.

Even at the Risk of Death

His cup would be His life. He asks the same of us. Not necessarily that we die, though there may well be things in your life worth dying for, but that we serve to the world our gifts and that we are prepared to pay the price. Leaders like Abe Lincoln and Martin Luther King Jr. ultimately did pay with their lives, as did many of the early Christians.

The day before his death, Martin Luther King Jr. talked about the cup. He mentioned an earlier attack on his life when a deranged woman stabbed him, and he marveled at all he had been able to accomplish since he survived that threat. He talked about the threats on his life that were still swirling in the air that day and some of the precautions that had been taken. Yet he chose to show up in Memphis and deliver a rousing speech on April 3, 1968, prepared to march for freedom the next day.

Nearing the conclusion of that speech, he said that although he didn't know what would happen to him with all the threats on his life, it didn't matter to him. Even though he wanted to live a long life, he'd "been to the mountaintop" and wasn't concerned about longevity now. "I just want to do God's will," he said.

The rest of that final speech, about seeing the Promised Land, is better known, but the main point is that he talked about serving up his gift, and like Jesus, his life as ransom.

Gandhi, the model for nonviolent protest that King used so effectively, had spoken of the cup as well: "There are many causes that I am prepared to die for but no causes that I am prepared to kill for."[1] He was aware of the price.

Perhaps your cup will merely be completing that graduate degree to teach at an urban college, practice medicine in Appalachia, or fight AIDS in Africa. Maybe it will require giving up a high salary to enter the ministry or care for a dying parent. Maybe it will merely be to get up an hour earlier to give someone a ride to work or take a meal to a sick person.

The Price to Serve

Going to bottom line, Jesus says, "But to sit at My right or left is not for me to grant. These places belong to those for whom they have been prepared by my Father" (see *Matthew 20:23*).

Jesus says, "Look. The prayer I can never answer."

You cannot pray for leadership positions in the kingdom of God. There is a prayer Jesus cannot answer. "You are sincere, you are praying, and you are serious," He says, "but I cannot answer this prayer. This prayer is not part of the deal. You don't pray for leadership positions."

So, you pray to be a manager. God says, "No, you don't pray for that."

You pray to be a pastor. "No, don't pray to be a pastor. No, no, no, I can't answer that."

You pray to be a deacon. "No, no, no, don't pray to be a deacon. No, don't pray for that."

"I want to be a leader." He says, "No, don't pray for that! Shut up!"

"Look, I can't answer those prayers," He says. "These places I cannot grant. There is a spot in God's kingdom that is designed just for you. It is a leadership spot, and no one else can get it. They can't even pray for it. These places are ready for someone the Father has already picked. I don't even get into that business. My Father has predetermined your spot."

When the ten heard what went down with James, John, and their mother, they were angry, but not because those two guys went ahead of them. They were angry because they did not think to ask first. It is called jockeying for position.

Jesus decided to have a leadership seminar right then. He called them together, and the seminar went like this: "Come, come. You know the leaders of this world," Jesus said, "They like to Lord it over people. Control people. They like to oppress people. Exercise authority over people. But it shall not be so with you," He said. "Instead, whoever wants to become great among you must be your servant. Whoever wants to be first must be your slave."

Matthew 20:25–27
25 Jesus called them together and said, "You know that the rulers of the Gentiles Lord it over them, and their high officials exercise authority over them.
26 Not so with you. Instead, whoever wants to become great among you must be your servant,
27 and whoever wants to be first must be your slave.

Then He said, "Look at Me. The Son of Man did not come to be served but to serve and to give His life as ransom for many people."

Matthew 20:28
"Just as the Son of Man did not come to be served, but to serve, and to give his life as a ransom for many."

Another word that the Bible uses for servant is *leitourgos* meaning "a public servant, a minister, a servant." This means to discharge an office at one's expense. You even pay to serve. This applies more to some politicians or pastors or business leaders. It means you use your gift to serve a country, a congregation, or a company at your own expense. The whole concept of servant leadership is that you are not doing it for gain. You are doing it because serving your gift is an extension of who you are.

True leadership always demands a price.

Jesus served His gifts so well to them that He cannot be erased from history. This is how people live forever in the context of human memory. If you serve well, history treats you well. If your motivation is always to protect the human value, rather than destroy it, history will always remember you well.

What Is the Price?

Leadership demands a high price. Often the more successful the leader, the higher the price. Some of the costs that you should consider as we move forward are these:

1. **Self–sacrifice.** A leader will no doubt have to give time and treasure, as well as forego many pleasures, rewards, or vices.
2. **Rejection.** A leader will find that people may not accept him or her as a decision maker, person, or friend.
3. **Criticism.** A leader will face scrutiny and analysis, because people often resent the one who steps forward or challenges their thinking.

4. **Loneliness.** A leader who dares to stand alone or who accepts a special role will find that isolation is part of the deal.

5. **Pressure.** A leader will be tempted to use position for personal gain, will be petitioned constantly to do this or that, and will be filled at times with self-doubt.

6. **Fatigue.** A leader will experience mental, physical, and spiritual exhaustion that come with serving and giving more of his time, energy, and soul for the benefit of others.

7. **Relationships.** A leader may see her family, friends, and colleagues suffer because of their association with her, and those close to her will have to share their loved one with others, as well as share the pains.

According to the biblical account of the last leadership meeting (*Matthew 26:23-25*), in that last meeting over dinner, Jesus accurately predicted that one associate would hand Him over to His enemies and another would swear three times before the night was over that he did not even know that man Jesus.

When our Leader went to pray about His "cup," the board members fell asleep, not once but three times, although He needed them to watch out for danger for an hour or so.

Matthew 26: 20–21, 44–45

20 When evening came, Jesus was reclining at the table with the Twelve.

21 And while they were eating, he said, "I tell you the truth, one of you will betray me."

44 So he left them and went away once more and prayed the third time, saying the same thing.

45 Then he returned to the disciples and said to them, "Are you still sleeping and resting? Look, the hour is near, and the Son of Man is betrayed into the hands of sinners."

They had failed at even small sacrifices, as we all do. Later, most of them were able to redeem themselves and become great leaders in preaching and spreading the teachings of Jesus. Sacrificing much, they traveled widely to form small clusters of believers to carry on the work and spread the teachings of their leader. Some even died for the cause.

If you desire leadership and accept the call to serve up your gift, now is the time to calculate what you are prepared to pay. Starting a journal or making notes as you continue reading this book will help you assess the cost.

Just ask:

What sacrifice am I prepared to make?
What price would I pay to be a leader?
What do these positions cost, Jesus?

8

It's Greek to Me: Out With Old Ideas

PRINCIPLE 4

INHERENT

"As a tree is hid in a seed so your future as a leader is not ahead of you, it's within you."

Our contemporary philosophy of leadership comes from the Greek thinkers. Our schools teach those philosophies in courses on management, leadership, or psychology and throughout the curriculum.

That is why schools make you read Plato, Aristotle, and other classic philosophers. They have to get those ideas in your head, so that when you come out, you will behave yourself and be a nice follower or an entitled leader. (It's also the reason why we have IQ tests, to separate losers from the leaders.)

When I was in school, teachers sent to educate us in the colony of the Bahamas had nearly dismissed me as incapable of learning. I was considered retarded. My teachers told me, "You will never learn." I was getting F's. It was common for us native Bahamians to be treated this way, and we rebelled.

From reading the Bible, however, I discovered that my leadership potential was inherent. I began making A's. That school where I was getting F's and that labeled me a half-breed monkey now has my books in its library.

When I was 15, I began to speak publicly and to share my convictions about the value of humans. Reading scriptures, I had learned to appreciate my own value. I understood that every human being is equal in value before God and in the family of humankind and deserves to be treated equally. That discovery came from my encounter with the leadership style of Jesus Christ, and that is the foundation of my entire life to this day.

Discovering my value before God and in the human family as revealed in the Bible enabled me to resolve my issues that resulted from living under oppression by colonial powers in the Bahamas. It resolved my issues with racism. It resolved my issues with segregation and discrimination. When I began my ministry in 1980 with a small Bible study, I did not want to become a pastor. I had a desire to share my ideas about human value. That idea attracted people to my ministry and allowed it to grow and touch people all over the world.

Gifting of the Gods

The Greeks and the Romans, led by great philosophers like Plato, Aristotle, and Socrates, believed that leadership was a product of natural endowment, of birth traits, of divine providence. The Greeks were the first ones to formalize leadership theories. When the Romans invaded them, the empire incorporated the Greek philosophies into its structure of government and leadership. The Romans became the most successful empire in history, ruling from Africa to London, England, and Scotland for more than two hundred years, using Greek philosophy as their leadership system. When the Roman Empire eventually disintegrated, its philosophies lived on as Europe flourished. As Europeans explored the Western world and spread their empires, the Roman philosophy dominated and still does today.

Throughout history, this idea of an elite based on divine traits has justified many atrocities: slavery, Jim Crow, the Holocaust, apartheid, sexism, and other manifestations of domination of people thought to be inferior or lacking in the divine traits. This philosophy maintains that leaders were born with certain natural advantages. It says the gods endowed them with a certain uniqueness that makes them different from the rest of us.

This thinking is simply wrong, outmoded, and not in keeping with Christ's model of servant leadership. Nevertheless, the concept exists in our seminaries. It exists in our universities, in our business schools, and in our political science courses. It existed in the colonial system under which I grew up.

To become leaders or recognize leaders, we must reject the old way of thinking and accept that all of us have an inherent potential for leadership.

Sitting in your chair, reading this right now, is one of the most awesome leaders in the world, and I will prove that you are going to make a difference in the world.

The Greeks believed that leadership is a product of charismatic personality—charisma. We hear this word often, right? It is of Greek origin, denoting "gift" or "gifting" and is also translated as "a gift of grace, a gift involving grace," referring to ability and empowerment. The Greeks used the word to refer to their leadership concept of being empowered by the gods and the unique position and advantage this gifting gave an individual over others.

Greeks used it to justify their leadership. They said, "Look, if the gods give you certain gifts, then you were born to be the leader of the masses." *Charisma*, they say, means you have special personality traits that make you different—for example, being an extrovert, one who is always up front, one who is always conspicuous, energetic, and well spoken. "Oh, that one was born to be the leader! The quiet one? Oh, no, no, no. Introvert? Oh, no, no, no. That is a slave. But this one? She has nice looks and she speaks well and she has a big smile—that is a leader!"

These are aspects of personality, and your personality has nothing to do with your leadership ability. Jesus never used the word *charisma* because the word represented a pagan concept. He never said, "I'm charismatic."

God Chooses the Imperfect

If you study history and learn about all the true leaders, their examples defy the traditional thinking about the charismatic leader.

God frequently used people whom others would dismiss, who were not perfect to do great things. Moses had a stammering tongue. No charisma. God said, "Tell you what. You're in charge of a million people."

Many questions remain about what kind of impediment Moses had, but obviously it had something to do with his speech because he complained to God.

Exodus 4:10–12
10 Moses said to the Lord, "O Lord, I have never been eloquent, neither in the past nor since you have spoken to your servant. I am slow of speech and tongue."
11 The Lord said to him, "Who gave man his mouth? Who makes him deaf or mute? Who gives him sight or makes him blind? Is it not I, the Lord?
12 Now go; I will help you speak and will teach you what to say."

The discourse came to a climax when he suggested that God send someone else to do his work. God said something like, "I am quite aware of what you can and cannot do. As a matter of fact, I have something to do with it as the Creator."

God did not heal Moses. That is important. Instead, He explained to Moses why He would *not* heal his impediment. He replied, "Even now your brother Aaron is on the way. He will be your mouth. If I were to heal you, Aaron wouldn't have a purpose in life." Moses always had his impediment, and Aaron always had a job.

Exodus 4:15–16
15 "You shall speak to him and put words in his mouth; I will help both of you speak and will teach you what to do.
16 He will speak to the people for you, and it will be as if he were your mouth and as if you were God to him."

Everything that you lack as a human is someone else's purpose. If we could do everything, then we would not need anybody else. The Creator did not make anything insignificant. Every plant needs the sun, fish need water, and human beings need other human beings. Each brings something to serve humanity. That is why servant leadership is so important, because it helps you constantly appreciate the value of people, and it also protects you from trying to devalue them by attempting to become all things and to do everything yourself.

Everybody is a leader. That is the heart of God. Leadership is inherent.

Under New Management

If anyone tells you that God told him to rule you, watch out. People think that because they have certain traits, they are better than you are. Jesus said the gentiles tried to Lord it over people or oppress people, demean people, devalue people, and then they tried to justify it by providence. That still exists today. People think that greatness is a result of pedigree—being of a certain class or occupation, being a certain color or being from a certain place. Jesus challenges that. His philosophy destroys the idea that only a few elite can be great. You will not be like the Romans, Jesus said, because they loved to Lord it over one another, but it shall not be so among you. For the greatest among you shall be the servant of all and the first shall be the last, and the leader shall be the slave (see *Matthew 20:25–27*).

He turned the idea of ruling others upside down, because true leadership is not measured by how many people serve you but by how many people you serve.

Defining Leadership

Among the traditional concepts of leadership are these:

Leadership is controlling and imposing one's will on people.
Or so the world teaches. But that is not leadership, only control! It is

manipulation and dictatorship. Leaders serve the needs of others and act in accordance with the will of God and for the good of the people. The greatest leader of all time said, "If you love me, you will obey what I command (*John 14:15*). If you what? Love Him. Not if you are afraid of Him.

Leadership is management of people. "You have to manage those people. You must manage those members. You should manage that group better." This is nonsense. People are so complex that you cannot manage them. They may fake it, lie and make you think you are in charge, but you cannot manage the human spirit. It is the most unpredictable spirit with which you can deal. You can manage things like machines and equipment and resources, but you cannot manage people. God never intended you to do so. Servant leaders manage things but *develop* people. You develop people, not manage them.

Leadership is superior to following. If I am the leader, then obviously I am superior. If I am the manager, then obviously all the staff must be less than I am in value. If I am the boss, then everybody else must be less than me. This is why the minute your friends are promoted they treat you differently. They were simply waiting for a title. They do not speak to you anymore. "I can't eat with you anymore. I have to eat with the other supervisors. I cannot have lunch with you anymore. I'm up in the executive suite." This is not servant leadership. Servant leaders value others, respect their function, and appreciate their gifts. The greatest is the servant, slave, youngest, and last.

Leaders are served by followers. Leadership is measured by how many people serve you. They say, "How large is your church? How many do you have on staff? How many aides do you have? You only have two? I have ten." "How many people serve me?" This is backward. I must be the servant. Serve your gift.

Leadership is cultivating and manipulating the fear of people. We develop the skill to manipulate people's emotions. The one who can do that the most and is more skillful is the leader. Therefore, if I can make you fearful and use that fear against you so you can submit to me, I am a great leader. The Bible says, "Perfect love drives out fear" (*1 John 4:18*).

You should not obey a man because you are afraid of him; that is dictatorship. That is not leadership.

Leadership is a product of providence. When a man believes it is God's will for him to be a slave, that man is in trouble. Providence means the gods chose certain people to lead; the others they chose to follow. The gods did it. The concept of divine leadership is a Greek idea. The pharaohs of Egypt had it. The Romans had it. The Greeks taught that "God chose me to oppress you. God establishes your position. You are a slave by appointment. I am a leader by appointment."

A Few Questions for the CEO

Just as this Greek philosophy permeated entire cultures, the thinking of a company or organization's leadership can spread to all within it. The question in the boardroom, when you are interviewing a CEO for the top job, should be, "What do you think about people? How do you perceive human value? How important are people to you?"

These questions are different from those we usually ask CEOs. We usually talk about their accomplishments and their experiences. Ask a CEO, "Tell me in one sentence: what is your philosophy of leadership?" The answer is very dangerous. The person may not even have a philosophy; or he might have one but not be able to articulate it, which is even more dangerous.

Hiring the kind of person who both leads and develops leaders requires that we do not ask the right questions.

To ensure that servant leadership filters down into the management system of the organization, servant leadership needs to be in every level of responsibility. For example, you have a director who has a servant-leadership philosophy but a manager who has a Greco-Roman philosophy. That organization would be in conflict, because the director believes that people have gifts and talents, but the manager believes that you control people.

Turning the Tables

If we can correct our leadership, we can correct our world. We must correct our leadership with the right philosophy and ideology, and the most effective, efficient, and viable ideology is that of servant leadership by Jesus Christ.

The solution Jesus Christ offered to oppression of His day by the most powerful imperial government in history, the Roman Empire, is servant leadership. It is amazing that He was born under oppression. He was born as a member of a colony of the Roman Empire. He was born as a subject of an imperial power, but His answer to the problem was servant leadership. He used the Roman Empire as an example of what happens to society when government does not serve the people. He said, "But it shall not be so among you." Good government focuses on serving the people, Jesus says, rather than being served.

I know leadership is not a product of divine birthrights. Remember, I was number six in a family of eleven children. In the poorest part of my tiny island, we lived in a wooden house with two bedrooms—one for my mother and father, one for my seven sisters. The boys slept on the floor in the room that also served as the kitchen, living room, and dining room. Our house sat up on four big rocks to keep the rats and roaches out. At school, my teachers told me I could not be educated: "You are retarded. You cannot learn." I survived, found my area of gifting, and claimed my leadership spot because leadership is inherent. It is in all of us. Servant leadership demands that we tap into our gift and give it to the world.

9

Check the Reservations:
Your Name Is on the Roll

PRINCIPLE 5
DIVINE DEPOSIT

"True Leadership is not a product of a course of study but a course in self-discovery."

W hen I used to arrive at a hotel late at night after a long trip, I would worry that the rooms were all taken. I have now, however, gotten used to my room being guaranteed by reservation with a credit card. My number is on file. Not only has my room been prepared, but it is also the best available, a luxury suite, the upgrade. I am often pleasantly surprised to find out that it has been set aside for me at the price of a standard room.

When a reservation for my late arrival is in the computer, the hotel secures a place for me. When people without reservations try to get a suite before I get there, the desk clerk tells them, "I cannot rent these rooms. The manager has already set them aside for guaranteed late arrivals." The manager often keeps some of the finest suites for this purpose.

"These places belong to those for whom they have been *prepared*," Jesus said when His aides were locked in a power struggle. You might recall from His conversation with Zebedee's family that the privilege to sit at His right and left is not His to grant.

Jesus said basically, "Look, God has already prepared that position, and I cannot give you anyone else's position."

Matthew 20:23
Jesus said to them, "...To sit at my right or left is not for me to grant. These places belong to those for whom they have been prepared by my Father."

A reservation for your leadership spot is already on file and the deposit is paid. A place has been secured for you. Your leadership spot is already reserved.

Leadership is a *divine deposit. Deposit* means "put there at conception." Every human being was conceived by divine prerogative to deliver a gift of service to humanity. It is by divine decree or providential decree.

Providence has placed in every person a packaged gift that no human gave him or her, but that each is supposed to give to other humans. Everyone on this planet is carrying a divine treasure that the world needs and that each is responsible for delivering to the world.

In God's plan, every human has a place set aside. Each is born to meet a need in creation. That is your place. God has *prepared* it for you. He has a plan to fit you, and He has built you to fit the plan.

To this end, we need to realize...

- Whatever the Creator calls for, He provides for.
- Whatever He demands, He supplies.
- Whatever He expects, He injects.
- Whatever He assigns, He designs.
- Whatever He calls out, He puts in.

When God designs a human for something, He builds into them the capacity for it.

People think that you have to get leadership from associations—

from whom you know—and from opportunities people give you. Jesus is saying, "No, you are being prepared in advance by divine providence."

To a corporate leader, He might explain that every human being carries within them an inherent gift given to them by their Creator, whether they manifest it or not. An effective supervisor or manager is one who has the capacity to help that person discover that gift and manifest that gift.

What God Had in Mind

Most insecure leaders present God as a stern master and killer, because they want you to fear them. That is not the nature of God. Jesus tells us, "He is your Father; your Father knows what you need. So do not worry about your food, your clothes; just seek first His kingdom, and His righteousness, and all the things you need shall be added as well" (see *Matthew 6:33*).

What a beautiful way to present God. He is a Father. He will pay your mortgage, take care of your tuition, be with you when you are sick, take care of your marriage problems, and even find you a good spouse to marry. He is a good Father, not a killer. Corrupt leaders may say, "If you sin, He'll kill you! Disobey me and He will kill you! God will punish you. Therefore, if you disobey me, as His representative, I must punish you or kill you."

Servant leaders do not cultivate fear or manipulate. Everybody is a leader, and great leaders develop leaders.

The Bible tells us that men and women might make plans, but in the end, the purpose that God has established prevails (*Proverbs 19:21*).

You might have many plans for your life, but He already gave you purpose. He already designed you with a purpose. Solomon was a great leader who understood that. He says, *"Counsel in the heart of man is like deep water; but a man of understanding will draw it out"* (see *Proverbs 20:5 kjv*).

If you are a corporate leader or small-business owner, when you hire someone, that person comes into your operation with a purpose that is like deep water, a gift buried deep inside. The Word of God says the man, or person, of understanding can draw that out of them.

That is a beautiful concept. My life's work is to help people draw out the deep water of purpose. Purpose means *original intent*, what they were born to do. Everybody is born to do something. A person of understanding—a leader—draws that out of them.

God has a plan for you, and He already gave you the potential to fulfill it. He gave you what it takes to claim your leadership spot. He built the capacity into you. He has high expectations for you, so He gave you the ability to carry them out. He designed you for leadership. He established a purpose for you. At one point, Christ even asked the disciples, "What are you so worried about? Look at the flowers. God has taken care of every detail. If He took care of them, He will do the same for you."

Luke 12:25–28

25 Who of you by worrying can add a single hour to his life?

26 Since you cannot do this very little thing, why do you worry about the rest?

27 Consider how the lilies grow. They do not labor or spin. Yet I tell you, not even Solomon in all his splendor was dressed like one of these.

28 If that is how God clothes the grass of the field, which is here today, and tomorrow is thrown into the fire, how much more will he clothe you, O you of little faith!

He has provided *you* to the world to fulfill a mission. He has given you the gift and determined a purpose. Not only that, He has given you the tools to carry it out and expects you to serve your gift.

He has already set aside a room, a place for you to serve your gift.

Buried Treasure

In life, the greatest tragedy is not death; it is living without a purpose. It is worse than death. It is more tragic to be alive and not know why than to be dead and not know life. If you are 40, 50, 60 years old and do not know why you are living, and still do not know your purpose, or why you came to this planet, know this: You were not born just to make a living. You are here to live out an assignment on this planet. You were born to make a difference in the world.

Each inhabitant of our world carries in them a seed of greatness to deliver to the planet. Greatness is in everybody. A good supervisor brings out the greatness in each employee.

Leadership is creating an environment that allows people to manifest their gifts for the corporate good. That is good business, and that is great leadership.

Many people die without manifesting this seed of greatness, however. They will take that gift to the grave without using it. They will be buried with untapped treasure. The wealthiest place on earth is not the gold mines of South America or the diamond mines of South Africa. It is not the oil fields of Iran, Iraq, Kuwait, or the silver mines of Central America. The wealthiest place on earth is the cemetery. It holds the treasures that people never served to humanity.

It is wealthy because buried in the cemetery are books that were never written. In the graveyard is music that no one had a chance to hear, songs that were never sung! The graveyard is filled with magazines that were never published. The cemetery is filled with businesses that were never opened. What a tragedy!

The graveyard is filled with visions that never became realities. The cemetery is filled with poetry that no one is ever going to write. Films no one produced. Ministries no one started. Dreams never pursued. Grants and scholarships for which no one applied. The graveyard is filled with ideas that were never carried out, inventions that were never mass-produced, campaigns never run, and sermons never preached. What a wealthy place! If I could mine the cemetery, I would be a rich man.

Someone reading this is a candidate to add to the wealth of the cemetery. Is it you? You may be getting closer to the grave without having delivered your treasure. You still have marathons you have not run, graduate courses for which you have not enrolled, and plays you have never staged. You keep procrastinating and putting off that dream. Some of you have planned to become "something" for twenty

or thirty years, and you still have not done it. You are getting closer to
the cemetery!

If you sing other people's songs but long to be a songwriter/producer,
God says, "It is time to write your own songs. Compose the music. Produce your CD. Sing unto the Lord a new song. Your time has come." If
you buy other people's art, but dream of painting your own, you need
to create your masterpiece. Bring out of you what is on the inside of
you. Do not let the cemetery take what is inside of you. Serve your gifts
to the world before you get there.

But You Have Potential

What do we call this wealth in the cemetery? Potential! The cemetery
is filled with potential. Potential is untapped power, unused strength,
dormant ability, unrealized success. Potential is who you are when no
one knows it yet. Potential is what you can do that no one knows about
yet. Potential is how far you can go in life but have not traveled yet.
Potential is who you really are but have not revealed. Potential is what
you could be but have not so far.

God is bored by what you have already done. Once you have done
something, God is not excited about it anymore. Potential is what is left
on the inside. God is a God of potential. God never remains impressed
at what you have accomplished. God is concerned that you are cel-
ebrating history so much that you do not have a future.

God is potential: *Omni* (all) + *Potent* (power, ability, strength). God
calls Himself all-potential or the omnipotent one. (Omnipotent means,
"I am all-potential.") Even though God gave life to thousands of galax-
ies, billions of stars, multiple planets, milky ways, He still says, "You
ain't seen nothing yet! I am still *all-potential.* I still have stuff on the
inside. I am omnipotent."

God works with the potential.

When God introduced Himself in the Bible, He introduced His
potential program. Then God said, "Let the land produce vegetation:
seed-bearing plants and trees on the land that bear fruit with seed in
it, according to their various kinds" (*Genesis 1:11*).

God says, "I have placed a seed of everything in itself." This is a mind–blowing concept. The last part of that verse, to paraphrase the Hebrew is, "I have put whatever something is supposed to be in the thing. I have put everything that the seed is supposed to become in it. Look, the seed of everything is in itself."

Genesis 1:12
"The land produced vegetation: plants bearing seed according to their kinds and trees bearing fruit with seed in it according to their kinds."

You were born with the seed of greatness in you.

Planting a Forest

You have no time left to sit down and look back at your past. God is say-ing, "Stop it! The seed of everything is in itself." Your future is not *ahead* of you. The future is *in* you. The future of everything is in the thing itself.

If I held out an apple seed and asked you, "What do you see in my hand?" you would say, "An apple seed." That would be a fact but not the full truth. The truth is I have a tree in my hand. That is, in my hand is the seed of a tree. In my hand, I have an apple seed with an apple tree that has apple fruit. In my hand is an apple seed with an apple tree that has apples with fruit, with apple seeds. You see a seed, but God says, "It is a forest!" In my hand is an apple orchard, a forest of apple trees.

God hides the future of everything in itself. In every tree, God hid a forest. In every bird, God hid a flock. In every fish, there is a school of fish. God is amazing. In every little boy, God hides a man. In every little girl, God hides a great woman. In them together, a generation, a dynasty of generations.

You are a seed in which He has placed a generation. The cemetery that gets your forest will not deliver your fruit. Men look at the facts, but God looks at the truth. Men look at the outer part of the matter; God looks at the heart of the matter.

When God looks at people, He does not see what you see. Your own mother does not even know you. Your father does not know you. They do not see what God sees. Christ asked His own mother, "Did you not know who I am? I was in your stomach for nine months. Did you not know?"

Luke 2:49
"Why were you searching for me?" he asked. "Didn't you know I had to be in my Father's house?"

My father is 83 years old. He sat in the front of my church not long ago, and I looked up and saw him crying. I was teaching, and I was wondering what was wrong with my dad. When I asked him later, he said, "I have eleven children, and I didn't know *this* was in my family." He saw the great ministry we have grown from a seed.

You do not even know your own children. Only God can look at a murderer, a fugitive, a killer and see greatness. Moses was a fugitive who had killed an Egyptian soldier for beating a Hebrew and then fled, but God looked at this killer and saw Genesis, Exodus, Leviticus, Numbers, and Deuteronomy. He saw a multitude inside of this man in the Bible. The next time you read Exodus, you are reading the writings of a murderer.

Exodus 2: 11–15
11 One day, after Moses had grown up, he went out to where his own people were and watched them at their hard labor. He saw an Egyptian beating a Hebrew, one of his own people.
12 Glancing this way and that and seeing no one, he killed the Egyptian and hid him in the sand.
13 The next day he went out and saw two Hebrews fighting. He asked the one in the wrong, "Why are you hitting your fellow Hebrew?"
14 The man said, "Who made you ruler and judge over us? Are you thinking of killing me as you killed the Egyptian?" Then Moses was afraid and thought, "What I did must have become known."

15 When Pharaoh heard of this, he tried to kill Moses, but Moses fled from Pharaoh and went to live in Midian, where he sat down by a well.

People can discount you, but God knows you on the inside. Only God can look at a dirty shepherd boy, David; a fisherman, Peter; and a persecutor, Paul, and use them for great things. God never throws people away. He knows what is inside of you. You are a forest.

Coming Soon!

Whatever you are doing on your job, do not let them destroy your forest. It is on the inside! Vision is when the seed sees its own forest. That is why you have big dreams. Your dreams are real. Do not die and go to the cemetery with them. Do not die without accomplishing your dreams. Some of you are thinking about retirement. God says, "What are you talking about? The word *retirement* is not recognized. It is not in My program," God says. "Keep working. Get busy and deliver your stuff."

God told Abraham at 75, "You still have something on the inside. This is going to be the best year in your life! You ain't seen nothing yet!" What you have done is OK, but God is disappointed in the things in which you take pride. God says, "Put your pants back on and get busy. There is no time to get tired now. Keep serving your gift."

I was driving in Florida, when I saw a dirty, messy property with dirt and mud in the front and bushes, dirt, and mud in the back. On the front, someone had put a sign with a picture of a beautiful building that said, "Coming Soon!" It reminded me that you might look at what is true right now, but God has planted in your life a picture that is already finished. Coming soon!

Dream No Small Dreams

Our dreams are built-in. You do not have to teach kids how to dream. They come packaged, but parents can destroy purpose if they try to make their children solve their failures. "Why do you want to study that? There's no money in that," a mother may say.

If your parents tell you that, tell them you must be about your Father's business.

If your child has a passion for music, buy him a piano. If she has a passion for painting, buy her some brushes and paint. Let the children follow their passions. You follow yours. Leave them alone. They came with their own assignment. They must be about the Father's business. Leadership is built in.

The first person to kill your dream is often your parents. They like to tell you what to choose for your career. They like to tell you, "Be like your brother or sister and go get a real job. Why do you want to be different? What is your problem? Why don't you just get a job like your brother or sister? (And be depressed like them!)"

Jesus said if any man is going to enter His kingdom, he has to become again like a little child. He means, "I don't care if you are 50 years old. When you come into My kingdom, I am going to make you go back to your childhood and see your dreams again."

Children are bigger dreamers than adults. Being an adult is dangerous, because we stop dreaming, and all we want is a paycheck. Children believe anything is possible. You ask a 4-year-old what she wants to be, and she says, "The president!" Your first response is, "Be realistic!" You are the one who is not being realistic. You have already stopped dreaming. The child is already realistic. The Holy Spirit has already told her that she wants to be the president. If that is God's purpose divinely deposited in her, it is what she should pursue. The position is already set aside. Do not kill your children's dreams! Jesus says, "Unless you become like a little child, you can't live in my kingdom" (see *Matthew 18:3*). Never grow up. Grow old, but never up.

I believe the redemptive work of God as presented in the Scriptures is not just the salvaging and redeeming of a human soul but the reclaiming of a forest with a destiny. That is why He loves you so much, because He knows what He put on the inside of you. Salvation means to salvage the forest. He did not save us to go to heaven; He saved us to do good works that were put inside us before the foundation. *"For we are God's workmanship, created in Christ Jesus to do good works, which God prepared in advance for us to do"* (Ephesians 2:10). So much is still inside of you.

You need to die as Jesus died—empty. On the cross, He said, "It is finished" (see *John 19:30*). It is amazing that Jesus never said, "I am finished"; He said, "It is finished."

He was referring to an assignment. He was 33 years old, and He said that He was finished—finished at 33. How are you doing? Can we be finished at 33? The answer is yes, if you knew why you were born. Age could be incriminating. If you are still living at 99, maybe you have failed to complete your assignment. Perhaps you are not finished. Maybe God is keeping some of us alive so that we can have some more time to discover why we were born.

Maybe we should die like the apostle Paul, who said, "I have finished my course. I have kept the faith. I have been poured out like a church offering."

2 Timothy 4:6–8
6 For I am already being poured out like a drink offering, and the time has come for my departure.
7 I have fought the good fight, I have finished the race, I have kept the faith.
8 Now there is in store for me the crown of righteousness, which the Lord, the righteous Judge, will award to me on that day—and not only to me, but also to all who have longed for his appearing.

"There is nothing left inside of me," he declares. "I served it all, and I am now ready to depart from here."

Can you die with joy? What are your dreams? Stir them up and take the gift out of you. Serve the gift to the world now.

2 Timothy 1:6 kjv
Wherefore I put thee in remembrance that thou stir up the gift of God, which is in thee by the putting on of my hands.

It's Just a Job, Man

God will never tell you to do anything that is not already in you. Some of you hate Mondays because you hate your job. You were not created to be employed. Your job is only temporary in God's eye. Your job is what they pay you to do. Your work is what you were born to do. Never confuse your job with your work.

You were born to solve a problem in the world, and you become more valuable based on the problem you solve. What you must do in life is find the problem you are here to solve. Find your place, your spot. Most of us are so busy making a living that we do not know the problem we are destined to solve.

You will become wealthy based on the problem you solve, not on the job you fill. If you want to progress on your job, identify the problems in the workplace and volunteer to solve them. Your promotion will come. Your company, church, agency, or school pays you for solving problems, not for just showing up. Your specialty is solving that particular kind of problem.

Do not work for money. Work for fulfillment. Society often tries to keep you away from your gift, because it wants you to replace your gift with a career.

God has given you a great gift, but the cemetery will take it if you do not get busy now.

What is your potential? What will you take to the grave if you do not make your dreams a reality? Have you fulfilled the purpose God put in you? Is your assignment here completed? The Father has prepared a leadership spot for you and placed in you the gift you need to secure it. Take possession of it.

10

It Isn't Yours to Keep:
Sharing the Riches

PRINCIPLE 6

NOT FOR YOU, BUT FOR OTHERS

"The value of all creation is in its contribution to others."

It was a cold winter day as I entered the aircraft and proceeded to my seat. A few minutes later an elderly man helped by a younger man came and sat next to me. "Hello," I said, noticing a plastic tube running to a transparent plastic cup over his nose. The young man who helped him to his seat handed him a cylinder tank, which he held close to his chest, as if he were hanging on for dear life. In a voice that seemed to gasp for life he responded, "Hello." I was tempted to continue the conversation but felt guilty about placing pressure on the man's capacity to engage in any lengthy conversation. Suddenly he turned to me with a smile under his plastic mask and said, "I guess you are wondering about this contraption here. Well, I am holding my life in my hands. This is my source of oxygen and without it, I would die."

For a moment I thought it was a simple answer, but then I suddenly realized the profound implications of his words. It is amazing how we can take the simple act of breathing oxygen for granted without realizing how vital it is for sustaining life on the planet. I sat there pondering his words and the aircraft rose over the tarmac and into the clouds streaming above the green carpet of trees and fields. I silently began to thank the creator for the green trees and every plant that provides us with life-sustaining oxygen. In this moment of deep appreciation for nature I suddenly was reminded of the truth that everything in creation existed for the sustaining of everything else. The plants need the sun, we need the oxygen of the plants, the plants need the carbon dioxide we produce, and the cycle continues.

This principle is also true in relation to every human being; you were created to serve an important purpose in the cycle of humanity and your generation needs you. Your gift is necessary for humanity. You exist not for yourself but for others. The essence of becoming a leader is discovering what you were given to serve your generation. Leadership is never for the leader but for those he serves.

My brothers, sisters, and I grew up in an area that anyone in the Bahamas would call poor. The minute you say the name of our community, Bain's Town, locals would immediately recognize it as a low-income area.

We were not aware, however, of how disadvantaged we were, because everybody else around us was poor, too, or worse off. My parents, especially my mother, who has passed now, constantly gave to other people. As models for servant leadership, my mother and father were the greatest influence on my life.

Being in a large family and having one parent working, you would think that our family's focus would be on our own needs, but every week other young kids from the neighborhood were in our house, eating our food. At least three times a year, my parents also would bring a large group of elderly people into our yard to feed them and give them treats. On any given day, my mother would bake ten loaves of bread.

You would think it was for us, but she would say she wanted to give those away *to guarantee our bread*, which was strange to us. This was a belief she had, that if you kept giving to other people, your needs would be met.

These were the foundational experiences that taught me the principle that when you serve others' needs, yours will always be served. Focus must always be on the needs of other people, not on your needs. That, to me, was the epitome of servant leadership.

Because of their charity and compassion, my parents became leaders in the neighborhood, not because they sought to lead people, but because they sought to serve people. Our family earned the respect of the community, not because they sought respect, but because they sought to respect other people and the value of other people.

Today, all my siblings are living off that experience. All of us have that same attitude that other peoples' needs are more important than ours are. Any one of my brothers and sisters would be willing to give whatever they have to help other people, because we saw that example in our parents. Whether a parent or not, a person who exercises servant leadership influences others to become servant leaders.

The Greatest Commandment

Maybe this was what Jesus meant when He ended His discourse with the disciples saying, *"Even I your master did not come to be served, but to serve"* (see *Matthew 20:28*).

He used Himself as the model to inspire them to emulate Him. Good parents and mentors do likewise.

Leadership is not for you; it is for others. If you wish to lead, you must serve. If we all discovered the gift God gave us and served it to the world, we could solve all the needs of humanity. I think that is what Jesus meant when He said that the greatest commandment in the law is to love God and then love your neighbors as yourself, as reiterated in several places in the Gospels. (See *Luke 10:27*: "Love the Lord your God with all your heart and with all your soul and with all your strength and with all your mind"; and, "Love your neighbor as yourself.")

How do you love your neighbor? You serve your neighbor. Jesus resolves the problems of humanity with one sentence. He says, "That's it; love God and then love your neighbor as much as you value yourself."

Servant leadership is the solution to the human dilemma. If our leaders in every arena of human influence apply the principles of servant leadership, they would have an immediate impact on their environment, their society. If government leaders were to take these principles and apply them, government would become what it is supposed to be and do what it is supposed to do: that is, to serve people, not just preserve government. If religious leaders were to capture the principles, religion would no longer be a mechanism used to separate people from each other or divide people, but rather it would bring them together to serve humanity.

The Servant Corporation

Even businesses can be servant leaders.

If corporations took servant leadership as their business model, how different would the world be?

When I visited Omaha, Nebraska, in the United States not too long ago, my host took me to see Warren Buffet's house. I was thinking, "This is one of the richest men in the world, but his environment is so humble." He drives a common car. He is involved in many community projects, and people see him drive the streets as a normal person, not chauffeured. He does projects for kids in the area. He still lives where he grew up in a house he bought in 1958. Most people move out somewhere, but he wants to be where the people are. I admire this kind of leadership.

He realizes that everything he has gained is for other people's benefit. That makes Warren Buffet one of the greatest examples in modern times of servant leadership. He is using his resources to improve the lives of other people.

In a similar fashion, I really admire Bill Gates, the chairman of Microsoft and co-founder of the Bill and Melinda Gates Foundation. He is more concerned about serving his gift than he is about being served by his organization. He is a good example of leadership. He seems more committed to following his internal dream than pursuing external expectations. This is where servant leadership begins, when you discover yourself and decide to pursue becoming yourself for the benefit of your generation. Your service to humanity becomes almost a by-product.

Companies like Microsoft keep coming up with new products, and the question is, what is a new product? My answer is that each new product is an attempt to serve humanity, to make work more efficient for humanity. The focus of companies should not be to sell products but to improve the lives of customers. Greatness as a company is a natural by-product of that.

Steve Jobs, the CEO of Apple Inc., is another example. He continues to use his gift to make other people's lives more convenient, more efficient, more effective, and his philosophy constantly drives his corporation. How can we improve human technology to make people's lives easier?

Anytime you serve humanity, success is a natural by-product. These companies may seem to be technical giants that are mindless of social concerns, but their goal is service. For example, when I first saw Jobs unveiling the iPhone, he never said, "Well, my organization is producing something important that will no doubt make Apple richer." Instead he spoke about "how we are going to make this easier for you to do, how we are going to make it more convenient to do this, and how can we make this do more for people's lives? Here are ten things that I am going to do for you to make your life better."

His selling of the product emphasizes what he did for the user, not what he did for the Apple company. That is a good example for all of us.

Of course, as soon as he unveiled it, many consumers ran to get the product, but his interest was not just in his company, but in serving. He uses his tremendous technological gift to make lives better every day. Benefiting others is what servant leadership is about.

Jesus always mentioned the fact that He was a *ransom* for many, not how important He was because everyone needed His ransom. He did not talk about how important He was to the world, but about what He wanted to do for the world.

My own experiences, my success as an author and as a minister are not about me. If you read my previous books, you will see that they are not about me. They are about making your life better.

Wal-Mart is another example. I think about Sam Walton, who founded the retail chain in 1962, after starting with a five-and-dime in Arkansas. His business model was "How do I get the most for the least for my customers?" Wal-Mart has become the greatest retailer in the world, and he became the richest man in America. He did not desire to become the greatest, so much as he desired to become the most effective provider of inexpensive goods to people. Wal-Mart is a simple example of the servant leader as a corporation.

In religious life, I see a great example in the life of William Booth, who founded a mission in 1865 that became the Salvation Army. His desire to take Christianity away from the self-centered aristocrats of Britain and to put it in the streets where the poor people were was what drove him. He wanted to provide for and serve those people. Here is a person who made an organization into a servant leader. It began with a person.

When organizations—churches or companies—begin to focus more on themselves and forget about the customer they want to serve, that is the day the company begins its demise. The death of an organization is when the present leadership becomes more self-serving and less a servant leader in the community.

The Master Demonstrates Leadership

If everyone becomes the servant leader he or she was meant to be, what would the earthly world look like? Look at Jesus' master class on servant leadership, the washing of the disciples' feet.

John 13: 5–9
5 After that, he poured water into a basin and began to wash his disciples' feet, drying them with the towel that was wrapped around him.
6 He came to Simon Peter, who said to him, "Lord, are you going to wash my feet?"
7 Jesus replied, "You do not realize now what I am doing, but later you will understand."
8 "No," said Peter, "you shall never wash my feet." Jesus answered, "Unless I wash you, you have no part with me."

9 "Then, Lord," Simon Peter replied, "not just my feet but my hands and my head as well!"

It is a model for how we might eradicate poverty on the next block or in the third world. It could be a call for direct ministry to those who have AIDS, those who are on drugs, or those in prison.

Christ's protection of that woman at the well teaches us about equality of women, among other things. Her conversion from instant prejudice against Him as a Jew, to become His PR person in that town, is a model for how we should overcome racism, sexism, and other "isms" that are alive and well today.

John 4:9

The Samaritan woman said to him, "You are a Jew and I am a Samaritan woman. How can you ask me for a drink?" (For Jews do not associate with Samaritans.)

The story also tells us to give others their due and sing their praises — no matter how different they are from us and no matter what we think about "those people."

John 4: 28–30

28 Then, leaving her water jar, the woman went back to the town and said to the people,
29 "Come, see a man who told me everything I ever did. Could this be the Christ?"
30 They came out of the town and made their way toward him.

Christ's lesson of the talents (see *Matthew 25: 14–30*) might be our wake-up call about stewardship over global warming, the issue to which Al Gore, the former vice president of the United States, has devoted his energies and for which he was awarded a Nobel Prize. This is an example of how servant leadership might apply in the world at large today. We have dominion over a rich planet. Will we leave it better or worse than we found it? Have we maximized the Lord's treasure?

Matthew 25: 14, 30
"Again, it will be like a man going on a journey, who called his servants and
entrusted his property to them....And throw that worthless servant outside, into the
darkness, where there will be weeping and gnashing of teeth."

Our dominion is over the things of the earth, but our leadership, our
gift, is for the benefit of others.

Without a Shepherd

One of the most profound yet simple assessments of humanity's condition that I have ever read is from the incomparable first-century philosopher and teacher Jesus of Nazareth. His observation of the state of
humanity, His assessment of our condition, and His identification of
the solution is found in one statement. Matthew, one of Jesus' students
and leadership trainees, wrote: "When [Jesus] saw the crowds, he had
compassion on them, because they were harassed and helpless, like
sheep without a shepherd."

This assessment applies to the condition of humanity today. The
same challenges and frustrations persist in every generation. The word
harassed used here means to be under the control or involuntary influence of external forces—to have no internal peace. Harassed means
to be a victim of circumstances for which you have no resistance.
Harassed people are trapped in a cycle of life, struggling to obtain the
basics: food, clothing, and shelter.

Our contemporary society has not changed much. Even the economi-
cally privileged in the most industrialized nations are harassed. We might
have even more stress as we "multitask" to keep up in our cyber-driven
culture: responding to our BlackBerry when we should be enjoying dinner with our families; checking our voice mail at home by calling on our
mobile phone from the beach, where we are supposed to be vacation-
ing; using our laptops on the weekend to tap into the office computer to
squeeze in more work on what is supposed to be our sabbath.

You rise early every morning, get stuck in traffic, go to a job you hate and work twelve or more hours. This is doing something you really do not want to do and for which you earn less-than-fair wages. You cannot wait to get off work, only to become stuck in traffic again. At home, you eat an unhealthy carryout dinner in front of the depressing news of crime and sleazy politics, and then you watch a "reality show" that is not real.

Finally, you take sleeping pills to get some rest. Too often, you climb into bed, lying back-to-back with your spouse because you are not speaking to each other, or you are so tired that just talking is an effort. Six hours later, you wake up still groggy and start all over again. You get through the day hyped up on overpriced, over-caffeinated coffee.

If you are lucky, you will work every year until you are 65 or 70, unless the company downsizes or moves overseas before then and leaves you or they replace you with a young person who has no experience but will work for less. You hope you will still have a pension fund, Social Security, and health insurance.

That is not life. That is harassment—one form of it.

We have professionals who pretend to be successful, happy, and fulfilled. They attract the six-figure salaries and drive the latest car. To get away from undesirable elements, they live in gated communities or penthouses. They take expensive vacations. At the same time, their family lives are shattered, marriages are wrecked, children are on drugs and birth control. The parents live a secret life of depression, fear, alcohol, or all the above. They are harassed. Poverty, hunger, homelessness, lack of health care, and a host of other evils harass those less privileged.

When you are harassed, life is beating up on you.

Jesus saw life beating people to a pulp. When He saw the condition of the people, He had compassion. He felt moved by what He saw. He hurt for them. He desired to help them.

A Failure to Lead

He saw humanity as *helpless*—lacking the capacity to generate change. Helpless means that you live under circumstances that imprison your hope and suffocate your will. This means you not only have problems, but you also cannot seem to do anything about them. The first-century crowds could do nothing to drive away the occupying Romans or relieve their heavy taxation. They could not wish away their diseases.

Jesus identified the cause of humanity's central problem: they are "like sheep." He did not say they *are* sheep, but that they are "like sheep without a shepherd." He could have said, "They are *without leadership.* They were in a poor state because they had no leaders or had defective leaders."

It is interesting that, in this instance, Jesus did not say the cause of their helplessness was sin or evil. This was not a "religious" description. He said it was the absence of effective, appropriate leadership.

Jesus Christ made this observation two thousand years ago in a culture where many people held powerful positions of leadership—the teachers of the law, priests, the Pharisees, King Herod and the Roman governors, Caesar. Those people had titles, positions, authority, power, and money, but He concluded that real leadership was absent. The ideas of philosophers such as Plato, Socrates, and Aristotle had been around for seven hundred years by then. Yet, Jesus said, in effect, "The people have no leader."

The leaders of the day had—either by design or default—failed the people. They had led them into a state of harassment and helplessness. The source of the people's condition was the absence, lack, or abuse of true leadership. After identifying the problem, Jesus told His twelve top leadership trainees that plenty of work was available and necessary, but few workers were on hand and ready to do it. Few were stepping up. Among other things, He was telling His students they needed to be workers in the harvest field—among the harassed and helpless humanity in need of true leadership.

Matthew 9:35–38

35 Jesus went through all the towns and villages, teaching in their synagogues, preaching the good news of the kingdom and healing every disease and sickness.
36 When he saw the crowds, he had compassion on them, because they were harassed and helpless, like sheep without a shepherd.
37 Then he said to his disciples, "The harvest is plentiful but the workers are few.
38 Ask the Lord of the harvest, therefore, to send out workers into his harvest field."

Leadership is finding your place so you can meet the needs in the world with the gifts you have. Jesus' students did not have titles. Yet He commissioned them as leaders. His instruction implied that we could change the human condition if we take responsibility to break the chains of the harassed and empower the helpless. It is an invitation to all, male and female, who wish to make not just a living but also a difference in the world.

Abuse of Power

Jesus said that you must serve yourself to the world, serve your gift. The leadership gift that you came to earth to serve is not to benefit you, but others. You become a great leader when you serve your gift, not when you prostitute your gift, not when you use it to destroy, oppress, or take advantage of other people.

Leadership is supposed to enhance, help, develop, and inspire others, not destroy, demean, and corrupt people. Of course, history is replete with those like Hitler, Mussolini, and others who found their gifts, but they used them for their own personal ambition, not for the advancement of humanity.

An example of misuse of power comes from Jesus' admonition to the same two disciples who sought to sit at His right or left. These two, James and John, were the first would-be "religious terrorists" in Christianity. They were the first ones He had to correct when they wanted Him to call down fire from heaven and burn who did not follow their particular system. "I did not come to destroy people's lives," He said.

Luke 9:54–56 kjv

54 And when his disciples James and John saw this, they said, Lord, wilt thou that we command fire to come down from heaven, and consume them, even as Elias did?

55 But he turned, and rebuked them, and said, Ye know not what manner of spirit ye are of.

56 For the Son of man is not come to destroy men's lives, but to save them. And they went to another village.

Jesus was really the greatest model of leadership, even when He was dealing with people who did not believe what he believed. His philosophy was that you don't destroy people. He said, "I came to save them."

True leadership salvages human life and human dignity. No matter what that particular human being may feel, think, or believe about you, you never destroy him. That flies in the face of servant leadership.

Leadership is not for our personal benefit. It is for the advancement, progress, development, protection, and enhancement of other human beings in the process of finding their own gifts to serve.

Religion that encourages or justifies the destruction of any human mind, body, or spirit is not in keeping with the ideals of the teachings and the principles of Jesus. Any policy, whether it is political or religious, that does not salvage human life is not servant leadership. Servant leadership is about salvaging humans, valuing humans, placing worth and equality on humans. It is not about superiority. The way some people use religion has more to do with *competition* than it has to do with *compassion*. Politics also often has more to do with self-elevation than the elevation of other people. Both of these strong forces need a heavy dose of servant leadership, so we can see solutions in the world.

We all focus too much on the irrelevant issues and ignore the most important issues. Jesus made a statement that if the blind lead the blind, they both fall into the ditch (see *Luke 6:39*). He was defining the value of their leadership. He was saying leadership is so valuable, that whoever is in charge will take everybody with Him, even if it is a ditch.

We have to make sure that we ask the right questions of our leaders: What is their philosophy? What do they believe? What are they doing that will affect our children and future generations?

Servant leadership is not only personal, it is social. It is public. It is national. It is international. It is global.

Servant leadership is necessary for the world to become a better place, whether it is our personal world or the global community. Leadership is for the benefit of others.

Who will lead those who are harassed and helpless?

How can you use your gifts in service to the world?

11

Leaders Are Made, Not Born:
Self-Discovery Is the Main Ingredient

PRINCIPLE 7

BECOMING YOURSELF FOR THE BENEFIT OF OTHERS

"Greatness is measured by how much of yourself you lose in
service to the others."

Trueﾟ success in life is not measured by how much you accumulate
but by how much you lose. A full life is determined not by how
long you live but how much you donated to your generation. In
essence *self-service* is greater than being *self-serving*.

I do not think I could have found a greater example of a woman
who wants to be a servant than in my beautiful wife and partner in
work, Ruth. She is the epitome of compassion in much the same way
my parents were. Every time I think of her, I think of the perfect spirit.
In that way, she has the same spirit as my mother, who was so generous
she shared what little we had with others.

Ruth always wants to make sure that people are comfortable and
have what they need. She is always working or initiating projects to
help young women, girls, or older people. Her compassion encourages
and inspires me. My wife works with all of my projects and is constantly there to be a support.

I met her when I was in high school, involved in community groups

to help other young people. She already knew who I was, though I
did not know her. Later, she also attended Oral Roberts University. She
was learning secretarial skills, which at that time were thought to be
a natural choice for females. In the community where I grew up, most
women were expected to go into secretarial work or nursing, or similar
fields.

In the twenty-nine years that we have been married, it has been
very gratifying for me to watch Ruth evolve. But taking a public role
did not come easily to her at first. She was afraid of up-front involve-
ment and quite introverted. Ruth never had a desire to be seen and
preferred to be in the background to help. Today, she is a public speaker
and she can represent me, if I am not able to serve. Sometimes she will
do a better job!

She has completely transformed because she simply wanted to serve.
She found purpose and acted on her desire to serve her gifts to the
world. This is the source of greatness. If you serve, you become great.

We misunderstand what Jesus taught, because our concept of *servant*
has more to do with servitude than it has to do with serving oneself
to the world. Our concept has to do with subservience. It has to do
with belittling yourself or making yourself inferior or less. That is the
opposite of what Jesus meant. He meant that the significance of your
gift matters so much that if you do not serve it to the world, you rob
the world of your unique contribution. He was not asking you to make
yourself less, but make yourself more significant by serving your gift.

True leadership is self-discovery followed by self-manifestation. It is
finding your personal purpose that you must offer to others. You must
learn who you are, and then reveal yourself to the world. This will set
you on a path of freedom—from the restraints of culture, society, and
other people, so you can become the leader God intends you to be.

No one else can make you a leader. You cannot decide to take a
course and become a leader. Greatness is not something you pursue.
Greatness is serving to the world what you discover in yourself. That
means anyone—whether you were a slave like Joseph, a jailed man
like Nelson Mandela, or a 5'3" Indian, who loved your people like
Mahatma Gandhi—can be great. None of these people fits the mold of

a great leader. What they did was discover the gift that they had on the inside, the passion, and then they decided to serve it to the world at the expense of their own safety and preservation.

Greatness in the concept of Jesus is discovering your true self and your true gifts, and then, humbling yourself, your true self, to serve. The word *humble* is from the Latin word *humus*, which means earth, "earthy." It means to be dirt. Humble also means to be yourself. It is a compliment.

How a Leader Is Born

People always ask me, "Are leaders born? Or are leaders made?" The answer is not simple. Perhaps the question is not the correct one. The question should be, "Are we all born with leadership potential?" The answer is, "Yes, we are all born with leadership potential and the capacity to develop that potential, but many will never discover, develop, or manifest that wonderful potential."

A leader can be born at any age. A leader can be born at the point of pressure, overwhelming circumstances, tragedy or disaster, or when an individual discovers his or her true purpose and passion. You may discover your leadership potential while reading this book.

If you are like Jesus and you connected with your gift at 12 years old, the leader in you was born at that age. Do you know the Bible story? His parents had taken Him to Jerusalem for the Passover. Heading home, they panicked when they could not find Him in their caravan. The couple went back to the temple, where they found Him in dialogue with the teachers, amazing them with His questions and His insights. He chided His earthly parents for worrying. "Did you not know that I must be about My assignment?"(see *Luke 2:49*). "Why were you searching for me?" he asked. "Didn't you know I had to be in my Father's house?"

His statement tells us He had discovered His gift. He was becoming Himself and taking on His assignment for the benefit of others.

Everyone was born to lead, but everyone must become that leader, just as one is born male but requires a maturing process to become a "man"—a father, a husband, an elder.

A seed is a tree. The tree is its gift to the world. But for a seed to bring forth its tree, it has to go through a process; the seed actually dies. For you and me to become what we are born to be, we have to put in an effort. The old self dies. Our greatness has to come out through the effort of serving. *Serve* means to manifest through effort. It also means to perform.

Gandhi, who used nonviolent tactics to free his people from colonization, understood the need for self-knowledge and self-manifestation. "What I want to achieve," he said, "what I have been striving and pining to achieve these thirty years is self-realization, to see God face to face...I live and move and have my being in pursuit of this goal."[1]

Most of the great leaders of history were not looking for leadership. Something happened that made them the leaders God intended.

Consider these examples:

- Jesus was a carpenter who accepted His assignment—that, as the Son of God, His real work was to teach a new way of living and then die for us. When He was arrested, He got His chance.
- Martin Luther King Jr. was a relatively inexperienced preacher and newcomer to the city when a bold woman decided to stay in her bus seat. The community leaders asked him to lead Montgomery's black citizens in a boycott to demand equality.
- Lyndon Johnson became a stronger voice for civil rights than most people would have imagined when he had to lead America after John F. Kennedy's assassination.
- Katherine Graham grabbed the reins of the *Washington Post* after her husband's suicide and took risks to protect the nation in publishing the Watergate scoops.
- Mother Teresa wanted to serve poor people in India and attracted others to follow her example, which ultimately brought her into the courts of kings, presidents, and popes.

Called to Lead

True leaders never seek leadership. A sense of purpose that reveals their gift and inspires others to participate in their purpose drives them.

Your personality type is not a factor in your leadership ability. Since every human being is here to be a leader, leaders come with all types of personalities. What they have in common is a compelling purpose.

Leadership in the lives of reluctant leaders or unlikely leaders often comes from these two sources:

Circumstances and pressure. Leadership comes out of crisis, challenge and the cry of destiny.

Intentional training and development. Leadership grows out of opportunities and projects.

The Bible gives us many examples of leadership. Remember Moses had a stammering tongue and no charisma. "Moses said to the Lord, 'O Lord, I have never been eloquent, neither in the past nor since you have spoken to your servant. I am slow of speech and tongue'" (*Exodus 4:10*).

God says, "Tell you what. You're in charge of three million people." God told him to go, taking Aaron to speak for him and the staff to perform miracles.

In a similar way, God picked David. When Samuel went to the house of Jesse in 1 Samuel 16 to find which one was the king, the father brought out seven sons—the charismatic, the educated, the athletic, the trained, the handsome, the cool—and said, "It's got to be one of these."

Samuel says, "Nope. Any more left?"

Jesse said, "Oh, I just remembered. I have my youngest son out there tending the sheep."

He said, "Go bring him in."

The little boy came in and said, "Yes, Daddy." Samuel turned around, grabbed a bottle of oil, and said, "There's the king."

Now David had a gift for using the sling. He discovered and refined that gift. When he met his brothers on the battlefield when Goliath was taunting God's people, he never thought of being great. He thought of saving his people and God's honor.

If David had chosen greatness, he would not have gone against Goliath. ("I will wait for an easier opponent," he might have thought. "I can beat someone my own size and everybody will think I am great.") Something deeper motivated him; and he knew that he had a gift he could use. Those with traditional leadership ideas tried to give him their gift of armor, but it did not fit. David said, "I have an inherent gift. I know how to use this slingshot."

1 Samuel 17:50
So David triumphed over the Philistine with a sling and a stone; without a sword in his hand he struck down the Philistine and killed him.

Our world has legions of potential leaders. We need to recognize and nurture the gifts in ourselves and in others. We all must achieve our own potential and help others achieve theirs.

Oprah Winfrey led a summer leadership class at the school she started in South Africa in January 2007. In a television interview, Oprah said she based her lesson on *The Wizard of Oz*—in particular the Good Witch of the North, Glinda's admonition to Dorothy that she had possessed the power to go home to Kansas all along.

Like Dorothy, you have had the power to lead all along.

Follow the Process

People who try to pursue greatness are usually not yet leadership material. To tap into that power and step out as a leader, you must follow a process. When Jesus told the disciples they had to become servants, He was describing a process. *"Not so with you. Instead, whoever wants to become great among you must be your servant"* (*Matthew 20:26*). Greatness is accessible to everyone.

We can dissect His meaning:
"Whoever" = Everyone, anyone
"Wants to become" = desires leadership
"Great" = powerful, significant

"Must" = is required to

"Be a servant" = minister to others, administer endeavors, meet needs

He says that "whoever" must follow a process required of all true leaders. If you want to be great, there is no shortcut. You must follow this process. Anytime you violate the process, you are breaking the laws of greatness. One example again is Hitler. Here was a man who had communication skills. He was an orator. He mesmerized people. In that way, he was awesome, but what did he do? He did not use the gift to serve humanity. He used it to control, murder, and abuse people.

Just because we find our gift, does not mean we know how to serve it. It can become destructive.

Toward the other end of the spectrum is the great Italian opera singer Luciano Pavarotti, who died in September 2007. Obituaries noted that he wanted to be a soccer player but had begun singing in choirs as a young boy. Soon his music took over. He had such a powerful gift that people wanted him to keep singing, and he wanted to do so. Known for popularizing opera, even more than voice or skill, he said once that he was a musician—not anything else—and cared about sharing his music with other people so that they could experience the spirit music provided for them.

He once said he entered the world of opera at a time when many predicted it was on its way out as an art form. In 1961, he had an opportunity to do the first "Live from the Met" telecast. The next day, people stopped him on the street. He realized the importance of giving everyone the opportuinty to enjoy opera—maybe even people who didn't know what opera was. The world came to know opera largely because he served his gift. He did not speak in terms of what singing did for him but rather what it did for those who heard it.

To Know Thyself

How do you begin the process? First, ask yourself, "Who am I?" Not, "What do I do?" Jesus never said, "I *do* ransom." He says, "I *am* the ransom."

To explore your spot and your purpose, ask yourself some more questions:

- Can I be a servant?
- Do I really want to be the slave?
- Am I willing to be the "youngest"?
- What is my function?
- What is my purpose?
- What is my gift?
- Does it bring me joy?
- Does it benefit others?

Other people cannot answer those questions for you, and you cannot take a course to learn the answers.

Other people will try to classify you, however. People are judging you all the time, pigeonholing you and trying to tell you what is best for you. Your parents will say, "Oh, I don't think that is a good career for you, honey. You will be broke." Your husband might say, "I think you should stay home." People will prejudge you and try to tell you what you cannot do. "You are not cut out for that." "None of your people has ever..." "But women cannot..." "Black people are not suited for..." "Christians are not supposed to..." "What would people think?" "People with our kind of money and breeding do not..." "You are too young to..." (Or too old, too poor, too rich, too something.)

People prejudge. They are prejudiced because they are ignorant. They prejudge something they do not know anything about. They think that if they can classify you in some way, they can cancel you out in their own minds. Many people you meet, at the bus stop, on a plane, in a classroom, in church, or at a social gathering—will immediately begin a process of trying to classify you:

- Where are you from?
- What is your family background?
- What is your political affiliation?

- What religion are you?
- Where do you work?

They keep prying in order to classify you and decide whether to dismiss you or not. But they cannot fully know you by these things.

Jesus' student John recorded an incident of such an encounter between Jesus and the woman who thought she knew all about Him. She was both judge and jury.

John 4:9

The Samaritan woman said to him, "You are a Jew and I am a Samaritan woman. How can you ask me for a drink?" (For Jews do not associate with Samaritans.)

She was saying, in effect, "I can't give You any water because I've already classified You according to Your background. Jews don't even speak to Samaritans, and we can't associate. Why are we even having this conversation?"

Jesus answered the woman from His perspective of a servant leader prepared to offer the world His gift: If you knew *the gift* of God and *who* it is that asks you for a drink, you would have asked him and he would have given you living water" (*John 4:10*, emphasis added).

"If you knew" is a powerful phrase. She thought she already knew who He was, so she prejudged Him. Yet because Jesus served His gift to her, she could receive this "living water."

John 4:11, 42

11 "Sir," the woman said, "you have nothing to draw with and the well is deep. Where can you get this living water?" ...

42 They said to the woman, "We no longer believe just because of what you said; now we have heard for ourselves, and we know that this man really is the Savior of the world."

I wonder how many people miss a blessing because they do not see the giver of the gift.

Jesus knew Himself. The woman was looking at superficial character-istics. Jesus told her, in essence, "You are spiritually, psychologically, and emotionally thirsty, but I'm a walking well inside."

When we really know people and their gifting, we change our attitudes toward them. When you discover the leader trapped inside you, you will see others differently, and they will see you differently.

Do not let others define you. You have to discover who you are and define yourself. Then you have to show people who you are and what your purpose is. Only you can tell others what your gift is and how you plan to serve it.

10 Steps to Self-Discovery

The first step in discovering your personal leadership is to recognize the desires the Creator has placed into your heart. If you know your desires, you can begin to identify purpose, which is the heart of servant leadership. Think about each of these questions carefully and answer them honestly. Record your responses.

1. What is my deepest desire?

What are the things you want most in life?

2. What is my passion?

What is the thing you simply must do? What animates and ener-gizes you? What makes you forget to eat or sleep?

3. What makes me angry?

What do you wish you could change about the world? What are the things you consider unjust, inadequate, or inferior in quality?

4. What ideas are persistent?

What ideas, inventions, or innovations keep coming back to you?

5. What do I constantly imagine?

What is your vision for your life or others' lives?

6. What do I want to do for humanity?

What problem would you like to solve? What need would you fill?

7. What are my recurring dreams?

What do you daydream about doing or accomplishing? What do you wish you could do if you could do anything?

8. What brings me the greatest fulfillment?

What activities, projects, courses, jobs, and hobbies have brought you the most fulfillment?

9. What could I do forever even if *there was no monetary compensation*?

What would you do most of the time even if you never earned any money for it?

10. What would I rather be doing?

What would you prefer to be doing right now? What would you do today if you had the day off to do anything you wanted?

Review your answers, highlighting recurring themes and noting how your answers fit into the picture of who you are and what you enjoy doing.

Consult With God

It is not enough, however, to look inward. While the process begins with self-discovery, you must also determine if what you have in mind is what your Creator has in mind. Many times when we fail at something, or things do not turn out as we would like, it is because we failed to discern God's will for us first. We did not check with the Manufacturer.

King Solomon and the psalmist David promised that our desires would be met if we glory in the Lord:

Proverbs 19:21
"Many are the plans in a man's heart, but it is the Lord's purpose that prevails."
Psalm 37:4
"Delight yourself in the Lord and he will give you the desires of your heart."

If you delight in your Creator and in how He has made you, then live as Jesus set the example, and you will fulfill your desire for personal leadership.

We have seen that every human being has a "prepared" place—a leadership spot where one belongs and can accomplish a purpose in life. Each one of us must find our true work to be effective and fulfilled. Your job is what they pay you to do. Your work is what you were born to do. When you become yourself through work, you serve yourself to the world. It is a natural thing. If someone asks you, *what do you do?* that is not the right question; the question should be, *who are you?* The greatest thing in the world a person should discover is not something to *do* but someone to *be*. True leadership is discovering who we are supposed to be. *Leadership is becoming oneself for the benefit of others.*

Who are you?

If you know the answer to that, accept your destiny as a leader, and understand the seven principles of servant leadership, you can move forward and begin to prepare for the practice of leadership.

PART 3

PREPARED TO SERVE

THE PRACTICE OF
LEADERSHIP

12

Believe: The Power of Philosophy

"No one lives beyond the limits of their belief system."

I f everyone was born to lead, why do so many fall by the wayside and fail to live up to their potential? The reasons are probably many, but self-doubt would rank high among them.

When I discuss leadership, most people do not think I am talking about them. I would estimate that 10 percent of the people listening to me or reading this book might be convinced they have some leadership ability. Ninety percent feel I am talking about someone else.

No, I am indeed talking to you! You must begin to believe in yourself, if you have not already. Let what is *inherent* but trapped within you develop and come out. It is time to change the way you think.

We have explored the seven principles of servant leadership, among them that leadership is inherent, Principle 4. However, many people believe leadership is reserved for the elite, an idea that derived from Greek philosophy and later spread throughout the world by the Roman Empire. This philosophy, as we discussed in Chapter 8, teaches that some are born to lead, and others to follow, and therefore leadership is reserved for a very minute, elite percentage of the world's population. The masses live in the shadow of the outstanding, gifted, elite few.

Even today, we, the average people, accept this philosophy. Our destiny derives from what others think of us. As we discuss how to prepare you for your leadership spot, the prepared place that the Father reserved for you—for each of us—what *you* think of you is key. What are your beliefs about you? What is your philosophy?

Philosophy is powerful. *Thought* is the source of philosophy. The word *philosophy* comes from *philo*, love, and *"sophy,"* to think or to know. It addresses our way of thinking, our system of belief. You live your ideas. You become your thoughts. Solomon says that what you think determines who you are: "For as he thinketh in his heart, so is he" (*Proverbs 23:7* kjv).

The word we translate as "heart" in Solomon's statement is a Hebrew word for "the center of reasoning." This does not refer to the conscious mind but the "hidden mind." Psychology calls it the subconscious mind. Whatever is stored in your subconscious mind is generally the real you.

Jesus of Nazareth said: "Out of the abundance of the heart the mouth speaks" (*Matthew 12:34 nkjv*).

He also said:

Matthew 15:18–20
18 "Those things which proceed out of the mouth come from the heart, and they defile a man.
19 For out of the heart proceed evil thoughts, murders, adulteries, fornications, thefts, false witness, and blasphemies.
20 These are the things which defile a man."

What comes out of the heart can be either constructive or destructive. Jesus taught that the heart gives birth to actions. The actions are committed there, and then they come out in deeds. His student John echoed this teaching when he wrote, "Whoever hates his brother is a murderer" (1 John 3:15 nkjv). People often think it is all right to hate someone if we do no physical harm to that person. Yet what is in our hearts tells the real story of who we are. Our innermost thoughts and ideas are hugely important because they guide our attitudes and lives.

Why in a book on leadership should we focus on the subject of philosophy? Philosophy is at the heart of our ideas on leadership. To improve or change our quality of leadership, we must address the philosophical dimension.

What You Believe

What others think of us is important, because we derive a large part of our self-image from them, especially when we are young. That includes what our parents think, what our peers think, and what our teachers think. We can even internalize what those who have never met us think.

If you hear something often enough, you might begin to believe it. Once you believe it, you react to life out of your belief system. If others tell you often enough and effectively enough that you cannot lead, you are likely to believe you cannot be a leader. You see through your beliefs, not through your eyes. Philosophy is more powerful than sight, because by your philosophy you interpret what you see with your eyes.

You can resist self-limiting philosophy with spiritual "re-conditioning," and your parents, your church, or mentors can help you develop a strong self-awareness that inoculates you from what the world thinks. The Bible says do not believe anyone's opinion of you. As the apostle Paul puts it, "Let God be true and every man a liar" (*Romans 3:4*).

Whenever "they" say, "You can't make it," "they" are lying. "You'll never be somebody." "They" are lying. The old folks say flat out, "The devil is a liar." The only person you should believe is God. You can do what God established for you. Anything less is a lie. If the car manufacturer built a car to drive at speeds up to 110 miles an hour, it can. If God specifies that you can lead, you can and you should.

Tell me what you believe, and I will tell you what kind of a leader you are.

I am not concerned with how many management courses you have taken, how much education and training you have, or even how many followers you have gained. I am keenly interested in what you *believe*—about yourself, other people, and the world.

Philosophy is probably the most powerful force in the world. Philosophy begins with thoughts or ideas—and ideas control the world. The power of an idea is that it can create reality. Everything begins with an idea.

Perhaps you are sitting in a chair right now. That chair used to be someone's idea. The clothes you are wearing came from someone's idea. Inventions, businesses, works of art, musical compositions, sports franchises, charitable organizations, hospitals, schools, and nations were all once ideas—concepts that became reality.

To have effect, ideas must be communicated from the mind of one person to the minds of others. It is words—whether written or spoken—that transmit those ideas.

If I have certain ideas in my head, I can transmit those ideas to you through the words on these pages. All the words we receive are "idea packages" that are delivered to us by the written or spoken word.

The great power of words is reflected in a statement made by a first-century student of the master philosopher and teacher Jesus of Nazareth.

John 1:1–3
1 In the beginning was the Word, and the Word was with God, and the Word was God.
2 He was with God in the beginning.
3 Through him all things were made; without him nothing was made that has been made.

Everything that has been made began in this "Word." The Greek term translated here as "Word" in English actually reflects a more complex concept than we might first think. The Greek word is *logos*, which literally means "something said (including the thought)" or "a word (as embodying an idea)."

Logos is the expression of an idea. To paraphrase John's statement, "In the beginning was the expression of the Creator's idea. This expression was with the Creator in the beginning and was inseparable from Him. All things were made by the expression of the Creator's idea." Everything—even our physical world—began with the expression of an idea. This is a principle that applies to all aspects of our lives, including leadership.

How Do You Think?

Ideas are vital, but our way of thinking about ideas is even more significant. When we receive ideas, our brains begin to work on them, analyzing them to see whether we accept them or not. If we accept the idea, our conscious minds take them and transfer them to an "account," called the subconscious mind, that stores them. If our brains do not accept the idea, we reject it and expel it from our thoughts. The accumulation of the ideas we accept becomes our belief system—our philosophy of life. These are the ideas we embrace, retain, and live by. It is our way of thinking, our system of belief, concept of truth, and perception of life.

All human beings are philosophers, because each of us has a philosophy of life, whether we realize it or not. Our philosophies are formed by ideas we have taken from others or have personally formed, which we have assimilated into our lives. These ideas help to create the reality we live in.

You live the ideas you accept. You become your thoughts. This is why thoughts and ideas are so crucial. People can make you who they want you to be, if you accept their words into your life. If you hear something long enough, you can begin to believe it and live it. If the ideas overwhelm you, eventually you might embrace them and store them in your subconscious mind. You become the thing people say you are if you accept what they say.

Once you believe something, you have a different experience of life, because now you react to life out of those beliefs. You see more through your beliefs than you do through your physical eyes. Philosophy is therefore more powerful than sight, because you interpret what you see with your eyes through what you believe in your heart and mind. Be careful what ideas you accept, because they can be either helpful or harmful.

On the one hand, the transfer of ideas can be hugely beneficial. For example, parents teach their children the value of honesty and self-discipline, and it stays with the children for the rest of their lives. A community passes on to new generations its values and traditions of helping the less fortunate and treating others with respect to ensure the continuance of a peaceful society.

The majority of us think we are born followers, and by design, the "system" keeps most people followers. Our political systems and our governments, even democracies, reinforce the idea that a few people will lead and others will follow. Every form of government in the world—whether it is Communism, Socialism, Democracy, or a dictatorship—implies that leadership is reserved for a few, so we do not even aspire to be leaders. Education produces followers. Most people learn to become employees, not business owners. We have few classes now in trades or in entrepreneurship. Entrepreneurs would be leaders. Entrepreneurship begins when people discover that they have a gift and pursue their dreams. They start businesses and build the economy. They build strong nations.

Instead, our schools teach students to get jobs and work for someone else. Students learn to be good employees. Even parents tell children, "Get an education so you can get a job." Most parents encourage this, without realizing they are handicapping their children's potential. The whole system is set up this way, whether intentionally or by default. Could they not say, "Get an education so that you can own a business or be an employer?"

The culture destroys the real you and produces the "you" that the power structure wants. This is why schools have a curriculum. A curriculum is a system to produce a product that is predetermined. The educational system can predetermine and predict what kind of person the system will produce if that person submits to that system. The system requires that all teachers study the same writers, the same version of history, the same philosophers, and so on — so they can produce more teachers just like them.

The average human being never discovers who he or she is. They become what everyone expects — except what our Creator-God expects. Systems of philosophy have sabotaged the great wealth of human ability in you and the people around you so that most people are achieving far below their ability. They do not know themselves. And no one else will know them if they do not change.

The idea of leadership that the master philosopher and teacher Jesus of Nazareth came to *reintroduce* returns to us the knowledge of who we are as human beings. His heart is that the potential and capacity for leadership is inherent in all people, not exclusive to some. This knowledge will change the world.

Then Came Jesus

Jesus Christ was the ultimate example of what a leader was not supposed to be under the traditional philosophy. He lived in a town with eleven houses and one street. He remained within the confines of a relatively small area during His life. He was born under Roman colonial oppression without any advantages, no high-society position. He was not even a Roman citizen. The Romans considered Him subhuman, second-class, a non-citizen. All the things that could work against a person becoming great were present. Even His best friends had low self-esteem, so He could not get His esteem from His associations. Yet his influence became global. How do you do that? How could a person with all those disadvantages and none of the advantages emerge and become the most significant person in history?

He says that it was not because He was the Son of God. Instead He refers to Himself using a term the Scriptures use frequently to describe Him. He calls Himself the Son of "Man," as if to say, "I am a human just like you all, but I used what I had in such a unique way that I was able to emerge above all of the disadvantages unscathed, and then lift others up."

Matthew 11:19
The Son of Man came eating and drinking, and they say, "Here is a glutton and a drunkard, a friend of tax collectors and 'sinners.' But wisdom is proved right by her actions."

Jesus Christ knew that every human being is a leader in an area of gifting. His concept is for each person to be a leader among leaders. The Creator created every human to be a leader, so we have a world of leaders. Each person has a place in God's human program and must believe that the place exists. All must be sure that they can function in that place and can contribute to their community and our world.

In order to lead, each must first become the servant. Servant leadership is not new, but it has been lost for so long that those who hear it today perceive it as new.

The philosophy of Jesus Christ concerning leadership is important because society's philosophies restricting leadership have not allowed leaders to emerge. Most have accepted the idea that they do not have the right stuff to be leaders. They have bought into an idea that is not true.

Jesus came to reassert God's plan. God created us in His image to have dominion over the earth, for leadership, and that leadership is inherent in all of us. Jesus reminded us that leadership is service.

The key to personal success is the discovery of your personal gifting. God designed and conceived you for an assignment. You were born to lead in an area of gifting, and your attitude toward life and leadership will be a product of discovering your gift and your function, so that you can serve it to the world.

A Can-Do Perspective

Until you discover yourself, however, self-doubt will contaminate your attitude. You cannot fake having confidence. That comes from understanding yourself—by self-discovery. You can read a thousand positive-thinking books and still think negatively. A positive attitude is a product of belief. You have to change your beliefs about yourself to unearth that trapped leader, the seed of greatness born in you and your area of gifting.

With servant leadership, intimidation disappears. When you know who you are, you automatically keep everyone else in perspective. If you think you are small and inadequate, others will appear large and threatening.

When the Israelites were about to cross the Jordan River and enter the Promised Land, twelve spies were sent beforehand to check out the land. The twelve all looked at the same inhabitants there. Ten of them said, "We seemed like grasshoppers in our own eyes, and we looked the same to them." The other two said, "We should go up and take possession of the land, for we can certainly do it."

Numbers 13:30–33
30 Then Caleb silenced the people before Moses and said, "We should go up and take possession of the land, for we can certainly do it."
31 But the men who had gone up with him said, "We can't attack those people; they are stronger than we are."
32 And they spread among the Israelites a bad report about the land they had explored. They said, "The land we explored devours those living in it. All the people we saw there are of great size.
33 We saw the Nephilim there (the descendants of Anak come from the Nephilim). We seemed like grasshoppers in our own eyes, and we looked the same to them."

Notice the ten said they seemed like grasshoppers in their own eyes. If I think I am a grasshopper, you look big to me. Thus, my image of you is completely dependent on my image of myself. That can breed fear. Let me assure you of something: 99 percent of the people you are afraid of are not worth it. They may even see you as a giant and themselves as a grasshopper. Fear is self-generated.

God had told the people to take the land because the land was theirs.

Instead of fulfilling their purpose, they believed they were something less than they were.

The result of oppression and negative reinforcement is self-hatred, self-devaluation, a sense of unworthiness, a lack of self-concept, low self-esteem, and self-destruction. They come from teaching people that they cannot do or become anything other than what society dictates.

Young people absorb what society tells them they must be. How many young men and women have said, "Why do I need an education? It's not going to do anything for me anyhow." Society has sold them an idea that their life is not worth anything, and their dream is not worth pursuing, so they quit school and join a gang that promises them greatness.

They are empowered as leaders in the domain of crime. They become antisocial. They hate society. They rob stores to feel the "rush" that comes from being able to dominate someone with a gun, even if only for a moment. If they go to prison, they do the same thing when they get out so they can enjoy that "power rush" again.

Potential leaders remain trapped, disillusioned, and confused. Yet, some of these same young people can extemporaneously compose and orate syncopated, original poetry *while* choreographing and performing original dance routines to complex, polyrhythmic beats. What if they could use those same skills in a productive manner to lead churches, schools, or nations? How much better would our world be?

Confused young people turn to crime to exert control over their lives. They desire greatness. Even the smallest child desires greatness. A toddler going through the terrible twos is simply expressing the desire for greatness. It is a struggle against adults for control, power. The two-year-old has not yet learned to use gifting to influence the world.

If every human being understood that one is born with a gift and with the potential to release that gift to serve humanity, instead of employment, we would have deployment. Everyone would start employing their gifts and talents, and we could deploy leaders to the world. Each person born of woman has a place in the world where he or she is supposed to shine.

Reflected Glory

Among the great problems of humanity is self-doubt. Those who doubt themselves do not know who they are; they try to be everybody else; they doubt their abilities; they put on other people's identities.

I have studied the life of Jesus for over thirty years, and He continues to intrigue me. He never automatically accepted others' opinions of Him.

Someone might have called you stupid, and you believe you are stupid. Perhaps you even quit school because of it. People might have called you ugly, and now you think you are ugly. Someone might have called you inadequate in something, and so you do not even try it anymore. What others say, you believe: that you cannot paint, swim, play the piano, do math, or—you fill in the blank—and so you do not! You believe someone else's opinion because you do not know who you really are or what your potential is.

It takes a completely secure person to ask others, "Who do you say I am?" as Jesus inquired of His students (*Matthew 16:15*).

You need to know the answer before you ask the question, because you are likely to get an opinion that is flawed.

Jesus came to give us back our self-image. But He could not do so unless He could show us what it would look like. Therefore, the Bible says God became flesh and lived among us, and we were able to behold, to see His glory. "The Word became flesh and made his dwelling among us. We have seen his glory, the glory of the One and Only, who came from the Father, full of grace and truth" (*John 1:14*).

We could see ourselves in Him. That is why we are so attracted to the man called Jesus and why we embrace His philosophy of life so readily. He personified every human's secret desire and aspiration to take control of life, circumstances, and situations—to lead life.

In the New Testament, we learn that two thousand years ago people followed Him because they liked what they saw. They saw what it looked like to walk on water, to speak to trees and watch them die, to speak to fish and fill a net, or to stop a storm. They saw the human spirit controlling the earth and they said, "I like that." For that reason, they followed Him everywhere He went, to the point of risking hunger, before He multiplied a few loaves and fish to feed thousands.

Matthew 14:14–21

14 When Jesus landed and saw a large crowd, he had compassion on them and healed their sick.

15 As evening approached, the disciples came to him and said, "This is a remote place, and it's already getting late. Send the crowds away, so they can go to the villages and buy themselves some food."

16 Jesus replied, "They do not need to go away. You give them something to eat."

17 "We have here only five loaves of bread and two fish," they answered.

18 "Bring them here to me," he said.

19 And he directed the people to sit down on the grass. Taking the five loaves and the two fish and looking up to heaven, he gave thanks and broke the loaves. Then he gave them to the disciples, and the disciples gave them to the people.

20 They all ate and were satisfied, and the disciples picked up twelve basketfuls of broken pieces that were left over.

21 The number of those who ate was about five thousand men, besides women and children.

He told the disciples, "Go out and do it." They went out, and they did it. They cast out demons, raised the dead, and healed the sick.

Luke 9:1–2, 6

1 When Jesus had called the Twelve together, he gave them power and authority to drive out all demons and to cure diseases,

2 and he sent them out to preach the kingdom of God and to heal the sick.

6 So they set out and went from village to village, preaching the gospel and healing people everywhere.

When they came back, they said they were amazed at their own success and effectiveness in controlling circumstances and exercising power over life's situations.

They said, "Look what we did, yes sir!" Christ says, "Do not rejoice because of these things. What is the big deal? This is normal for you." He says what you should rejoice in is that you reconnected to heaven. Now your name is back in the book. You should rejoice over that. You are back in touch with your Manufacturer.

You merely did what the Master expected of you. The Bible implies that merely carrying out the normal duties of leadership is not cause for great praise. It is supposed to be natural. Leadership is your nature. It's genetic.

Luke 17:7–10

7 Suppose one of you had a servant plowing or looking after the sheep. Would he say to the servant when he comes in from the field, "Come along now and sit down to eat"?

8 Would he not rather say, "Prepare my supper, get yourself ready and wait on me while I eat and drink; after that you may eat and drink"?

9 Would he thank the servant because he did what he was told to do?

10 So you also, when you have done everything you were told to do, should say, "We are unworthy servants; we have only done our duty."

Note carefully that this scripture states that your leadership service is your "duty"—not an issue of exception. When you are exercising and serving your gift to the world, you are doing what is natural and expected, so praise and applause are not necessary. Just like a servant, we are expected to serve. Essentially, true leaders do not work for recognition, appreciation, accolades, or pride, but as an obligation to humanity. In other words, leadership to a true leader is a privilege, not a right. True servant leadership, therefore, is seen as a duty one has to humanity. Wow! What a difference this philosophy would make in the marketplace of life.

Move the Mountain!

Jesus urges us to believe we can do more than the ordinary, even more than the extraordinary. He tells humanity to believe. Let me just caution, however, that belief is not enough, because you can believe the wrong thing. He qualifies it by prescribing whom you should believe. Believe what God says about you. He is the Creator. Believe the Maker, not other people's opinions.

One day, Jesus spoke to a tree, and the disciples became shocked. He said, in essence, "Why do you worry about speaking to a tree? You could speak to mountains."

Matthew 21:18–22

18 Early in the morning, as he was on his way back to the city, he was hungry.
19 Seeing a fig tree by the road, he went up to it but found nothing on it except leaves. Then he said to it, "May you never bear fruit again!" Immediately the tree withered.
20 When the disciples saw this, they were amazed. "How did the fig tree wither so quickly?" they asked.
21 Jesus replied, "I tell you the truth, if you have faith and do not doubt, not only can you do what was done to the fig tree, but also you can say to this mountain, 'Go, throw yourself into the sea,' and it will be done.
22 If you believe, you will receive whatever you ask for in prayer."

He more or less said, "You have fallen so low from who you really used to be that being natural is exceptional. My speaking to a tree shocks you, but you have the power to speak to a mountain."

God is not impressed when you cast out a demon. God is not impressed when we take authority over the germ of tuberculosis or take authority over the AIDS virus. God is not surprised and shocked when you bind and loose and cast out disease and infirmity.

Jesus says you can speak to that mountain, tell it to move and go into the sea. That takes a God kind of faith. Say it: "Go! In the name of Jesus, by the authority of my image, go! Crawl into the sea! Go away in the name of Jesus! Mountain, get out of my way, I say."

Believe it.

One old song says, "You don't have to move the mountain. Just give me strength to climb." Forget that, you can move the mountain!

You have to say it until the mountain is history. Have you heard people use the acronym P.U.S.H.—Pray Until Something Happens? Push the mountain. You have the power to do that. Whatever He calls you for, you can do. First, you have to believe. The Bible says you only need faith the size of a tiny seed, the mustard seed:

> He replied, "Because you have so little faith. I tell you the truth, if you have faith as small as a mustard seed, you can say to this mountain, 'Move from here to there' and it will move. Nothing will be impossible for you" (*Matthew 17:20*).

I Am a Leader

It is not easy reversing years of not being trained to believe in yourself, but you can nurture that belief, reminding yourself you can do anything.

Greatness is separating yourself from other people's opinions of you. Greatness is delivering yourself from people's expectations of you. Greatness is discovering that you are more than what society thought you were.

To help you achieve greatness, I have adapted these affirmations from some of my earlier writings. Read them periodically to help maximize your potential to lead:

Affirmations

1. **I possess a deep, guiding purpose,** the meaning and the reason for my existence.
2. **I have a clear vision,** a personal and a corporate vision that I can communicate to others.
3. **I love to serve others** with a passion to see their lives improve and to help them maximize their potential and develop their own leadership.
4. **I have established clear goals** in accordance with my gift and God's purpose for me.
5. **I cultivate my spiritual reserves** through Scripture, prayer, and faith practices.

6. **I am teachable,** as I demonstrate through study, reading, listening to those from whom I can learn, and benefiting from my mistakes.

7. **I am constantly refining my skills** through practice, innovation, and adaptation to achieve excellence.

8. **I believe in others** and value their worth, their differences, and their weaknesses.

9. **I am bold and decisive,** trusting in my strengths and my inherent, God-given leadership.

10. **I have integrity** in all my dealings with people.

11. **I maximize my opportunities** and my time to achieve results.

12. **I am a leader** created in the image of God and committed to serving my gifts.

13

Prepare: The Toolbox of a Leader

"Ability without skill is the source of mediocrity."

If I was born to lead, why do I have to prepare for it?"

You would be justified in asking that. Preparation is necessary before one undertakes any endeavor. You might have the capacity to do a task and the potential for success, but to achieve it you will need some tools. The Savior's admonition that "whoever wants to *become* great" implies a process of preparation (*Matthew 20:26*, emphasis added).

Without some training, your chances of fulfilling your purpose are slim. Whosoever becomes the CEO probably spent some time as the intern.

While leadership is inherent, success at it will require some preparation, study, prayer, or contemplation. To carry out the mission, orders, or contract, a leader must have some assets.

Are there characteristics that effective leaders have in common? If you studied the lives of great leaders—even those in your company or neighborhood who run a staff, a team, or a family—you would probably be able to list some similarities.

At the top of the list is probably the ability to inspire. Leaders inspire. To inspire is to activate, to mobilize. To inspire is to make others internalize your decisions, your values or your goals.

Leaders who cannot inspire people often try to manipulate them, but true leadership is setting an example for others to emulate because they are inspired. Those who play on people's fears, threaten, promise, or coerce are not leaders; they are professional manipulators. Their aim is to control, oppress, dictate.

What is the difference? If I order you to do something and I threaten you with consequences—perhaps a pay cut, a demotion, or even violence—that is coercion. If I lead by example, if I make you want to do what I ask you to do, that is inspirational leadership. If I wash the feet of my friends and co-workers, as Jesus did to demonstrate servant leadership, and I urge you to do likewise for others, and you do, that is inspiration at work.

The Breath of God

The meaning of the word *inspire* comes from the Latin for *inhale*—"to breathe in." The Hebrew word for *inspire* means "God's breath."

Our Maker breathes the capacity into us. Inspiration is the very breath of a leader. Inspiration is as critical as the air we breathe. It is so critical it defines true leadership. In this book, our working definition of leadership is:

Leadership is the capacity to influence others through inspiration generated by a passion, motivated by a vision, birthed by a conviction, produced by a purpose.

Let us review these key words:

Influence
Inspiration
Passion
Vision

Conviction
Purpose

The fundamental evidence of true leadership is influence. The essence of leadership is influence. Again, influence can be confused with or mistaken for manipulation.

To lead anyone anywhere or to get someone to do something, you must influence him or her. As a servant leader, threats and oppression are not options for you. You have a better chance of influencing others if you can inspire them. You inspire them through your own passion for the task or the subject.

Most parents do not inspire their children. They manipulate them or order them to do things. They threaten or harass to try to control them and often fail. If you want to inspire your children to read, for example, then you must first develop a passion for books. If you tell your kid, "Don't watch TV," but they see you spending hours watching it, they will too. If, instead, they see you buying books or newspapers and spending hours reading instead of watching television, they may be inspired to read. Whatever you are passionate about inspires others.

That is the heart of leadership. Passion produces inspiration. If you can inspire people, you can influence them. Through inspiration, a leader can motivate followers to rearrange their priorities for the sake of a greater vision.

Oprah Winfrey is an example of someone who leads by inspiration. While her humble beginnings might have been an impediment to others, they appear to be a stabilizer in her present life. Maybe that is why she still has the knack for giving things away, helping people, and building schools. She is always doing projects and assisting people. I believe it is her way of staying in touch with herself, and she is a great inspiration, especially to women who see her as a symbol of what you can accomplish. At the same time, I think women are attracted to her because she likes to serve. She has a nurturing spirit, a great example of servant leadership. An inspired leader, she influences people.

A Reason for Being

So where does passion come from? How do we get this kind of passion?

Passion is motivated by a vision, birthed from a conviction, and produced by a sense of purpose.

The first thing you need to do is discover your purpose. Purpose is original intent. You have to find out the original intent for your life. The word *purpose* means reason for creation: "To intend, resolve or plan." Purpose is the reason for which we exist, the thing the Creator sent us to do.

We accomplish our purpose through persistence and perseverance. Passion, a deep desire and commitment fuel purpose.

Leaders do not pursue leadership, because they are busy pursuing their purpose. True leaders do not pursue followers; followers are attracted to true leaders. Leadership is a noble privilege given by inspired followers, in partnership to accomplish a shared vision. Conviction, passion, and purpose attract others to designate a leader. True leadership has very little to do with pursuing and securing followers and more to do with personally pursuing a sense of purpose. The source of successful leadership is this resolute passion for a vision, fueled by a conviction that produces a sense of obligation. In essence, a leader is willing to pursue his purpose even if she or he has to go it alone. Perhaps this is why true leaders are internally motivated. They go toward their dream even without "followers." If a leader is not willing to pursue his or her purpose with a passion deep enough to go it alone, that leader is not worthy to be followed.

Mother Teresa used to say, "Do not wait for leaders. Do it alone, person to person."

The other leaders might not show up. You are a leader alone in your passion and conviction. When you discover your personal passion and are willing to pursue it at all cost, a leader is born.

Leadership is the discovery of a purpose and vision that drive the visionary *beyond the boundary of personal preservation*. Vision produces true leaders. Vision separates leaders from managers.

All visions have only one believer at first. Everyone who dares to cultivate leadership will have his or her vision tested. The time will come when no one else believes in your purpose but you. Leadership will be like that sometimes.

The only person who knows your purpose is God. Everything that exists, including the shoes on your feet and the chair upon which you sit, has a purpose, but the original purpose for that thing is in the mind of the Manufacturer. If you do not know your Manufacturer, it will be difficult at best to determine your purpose. Your life will have no meaning without a relationship with God, because He is the only One who knows why He conceived you. Until you learn why God made you, you are a follower.

To discover God's purpose, you will also need His manual for us, the Bible. One of the most powerful scriptures I have ever read holds the key to life. It says, "Many are the plans in a man's heart, but it is the Lord's purpose that will prevail" (*Proverbs 19:21*).

This verse teaches us three things:

Purpose is more important than plans.
Purpose is more powerful than plans.
Purpose precedes plans.

Look at God's mind again. God says that many are the plans in a man's heart but God's purpose will prevail over all plans. It means God is not too interested in your plans. He is interested in His *purpose* for your life. The word *plan* means "schemes, ideas, and devices." You come up with your own ideas of what you want to be, what you want to do, where you want to go, where you want to live, where you want to move, whom you want to be with, where you want to go on a vacation, what you want to study as a career. God is saying, however, "Wait a minute, come to Me first."

How many have gone to college and earned a degree in the wrong thing? They went to college before they went to God. They made their own plans. Then they had to run to God when their plans did not come to fruition. God is saying, "Before you make plans for your life, consult Me for your purpose." Plans are what you create. Purpose is what

God establishes, so to God, purpose is more important than plans. Your plans should come from God's purpose.

When you discover your purpose, you become immune to your past. When you discover your purpose, you become immune to opposition. It is like a seed that has been germinated. Have you ever seen a plant that broke up concrete to grow through it — a tree sticking up through a sidewalk or parking lot? Maybe you have seen a tree that bends around a barrier and continues to grow on the other side. That is how it is when you find your purpose. You push through anything or go around any obstacle to pursue your vision. No matter what people do to try to hold you down, they cannot because you have purpose. The purpose inside of you is your driving force. You are unstoppable. Nothing can hold you down.

Paul said, "For this purpose I was appointed a herald and an apostle" to the Gentiles (1 Timothy 2:7). He knew his purpose.

Who is a leader?

Leaders are simply people who have discovered themselves and decided to become who they really are.

Leaders are simply people who dare to be who the Creator made them to be and are committed to expressing themselves fully to the world through their gifts.

The Strength of Your Convictions

The next step is developing conviction. Once you discover your purpose, it becomes a conviction. You begin to believe that you were born to do this thing. That is why leaders can seem possessed. They become self-possessed.

What was the conviction that made us follow Nelson Mandela? His conviction that humans are equal was so strong that the government sent him to prison. The Rev. Dr. Martin Luther King Jr. also went to jail repeatedly and used the experience to make his point. Jesus was arrested, tried, and executed. What is great about the gift of conviction is that the jailer can lock it up but not destroy it.

Purpose is more powerful than problems. It is more powerful than opposition, more powerful than criticism. Criticism can be proof that you are moving toward your purpose. Your purpose separates you from the crowd. Folks who are going nowhere want you to be just like them. Those who are doing nothing want you to do it with them. When you discover your purpose, you also discover your enemy, and sometimes it is in your own house. Your mother, father, spouse, or child may oppose you and become an obstacle. You keep pressing on because you have purpose and conviction.

Conviction leads to passion. A leader is a passionate person. When you find your purpose, you develop a passion for it. When you have a passion, you will work on it without stopping, sometimes without eating, without sleeping, without taking weekends off. It is your leadership spot. You are in the zone. If you look at your watch more than you look at your future, however, you are a follower.

True leaders set no time limit on performance. They are motivated by finishing. *"It is finished,"* said Jesus. The reward is in the assignment. They do not care about pay or overtime. They work for themselves, not for the monetary reward. If you are ready to clock out every day at five o'clock, you are not a leader in your workplace. You are an employee. A follower. Perhaps that is not your spot.

The Mind of a Leader

When leaders discover their passion, they begin to develop strange behaviors. The first one is a positive attitude, because your passion gives you hope. Your purpose gives you answers to life. You suddenly realize, "Wow! I was born to do something about something. I was born to do this!" Everyone is an answer to a question. You were born to answer a question on earth, and that gives a leader a positive attitude. What were you born to do? People who have discovered their purpose are rarely depressed. They may get discouraged, because they have big dreams. They are not depressed, though, because they know what they are going to do next. There is a difference between being depressed and discouraged.

People who know their purpose are never bored. Their greatest complaint is that twenty-four hours is not enough hours in a day because they have found something that is bigger than life. When people say they are bored, the people with purpose wonder why the others cannot find anything to do.

The Bible talks about hating sleep. A great man, a man of purpose, hates sleep—too much sleep and you become poor. "Do not love sleep or you will grow poor; stay awake and you will have food to spare" (*Proverbs 20:13*).

When you find your purpose and develop a passion for it, you may actually hate weekends because the break interferes with your momentum and energy. One time, Jesus' students, knowing He was tired from a journey, urged Him to eat some food they had gotten from a nearby town:

John 4:32–35
32 He said to them, "I have food to eat that you know nothing about."
33 Then his disciples said to each other, "Could someone have brought him food?"
34 "My food," said Jesus, "is to do the will of him who sent me and to finish his work.
35 Do you not say, 'Four months more and then the harvest'? I tell you, open your eyes and look at the fields! They are ripe for harvest."

Jesus was so passionate about His purpose that it was more important than food to Him. When you find something to do that is more important than your mealtimes, you are becoming a leader. If you cannot skip lunch or be late for dinner, perhaps you are not the leader you need to be yet.

Passion inspires others. The passion comes from your vision. You see a plan to carry out your purpose. You see what can result from the mission. You envision the end product, and you can sell others on helping you accomplish it.

Ronald Reagan, the former United States president, had a passion to see those oppressed by Communist ideology set free. The desire to see those people liberated moved him so much that he made a statement to the leader of the Soviet Union that did not seem necessarily political for someone in his position: "Tear down this wall."

A politician is not supposed to say that, but at that moment, he was no longer a politician. He was really a civil rights leader. We do not think of him that way, and we do not always appreciate the significance of what he did. He caused the dismantling of that regime, and the freeing of millions of people. He was serving the interest of other people, and that is why he is so significant. No, he did not balance the budget. He did not necessarily produce a strong economy, but he changed the world. History, therefore, will probably treat him in a positive manner. He is one of those modern leaders whom I admire as an example of serving yourself to the world. You have to take risks as a leader, and he took that great risk of stepping out and doing something that no one thought was possible. And it *was* possible. He brought passion to the task.

Better Than Money

Some of the greatest leaders in the world are those who lead charitable organizations. When people are not paid to serve, they must have some other reason to do it. Leading that kind of organization demands a passion. It demands a conviction.

You have to gain people's commitment without money. People have to work for you because they want to be involved. You have to have something better than money, like inspiration. Jesus never paid the disciples any money, but they left their businesses to follow Him.

Matthew 4:18–22

18 As Jesus was walking beside the Sea of Galilee, he saw two brothers, Simon called Peter and his brother Andrew. They were casting a net into the lake, for they were fishermen.

19 "Come, follow me," Jesus said, "and I will make you fishers of men."

20 At once they left their nets and followed him.
21 Going on from there, he saw two other brothers, James son of Zebedee and his brother John. They were in a boat with their father Zebedee, preparing their nets. Jesus called them,
22 and immediately they left the boat and their father and followed him.

One example of inspiring someone to do the work you have in mind involves some of the richest people in the world. Bill and Melinda Gates built a foundation that spends billions to solve global problems. They do so using innovative thinking and methods, applying not only their fortune but also wisdom they gained from the business world while running Microsoft. Through the foundation, they wield tremendous influence. That would be admirable enough and a good example of servant leadership, but the big story is that they inspired Warren Buffet, another one of the richest business leaders, to give the foundation billions of his dollars to use toward its purpose.

He was impressed with the way they managed their domain, and he saw no need to reinvent the horse by creating something of his own. That is the fruit of inspiration. He could have kept the money. He could have found a deserving relative, friend, or another cause, but Buffet not only shared the Gates's purpose and passion, but he also bought into their vision.

Another example of a servant leader was Jimmy Carter. Many people did not admire him or consider him the greatest U.S. president, but he was a leader with compassion. At the very least, he wanted to provide decent houses for people. I have little doubt that he brings value to people. His compassion is evident, and I admire that in him. He is still often called on to work on behalf of the nation because of that quality of compassion and passion that people sense in him.

Another example of a servant leader is Billy Graham, the evangelist who dedicated his life to improving other people's lives. Everything he did was to seek the value of a person's soul. He gave himself to his ministry. Even America's presidents called him to minister to them personally.

All of these leaders had purpose and passion. All of them inspired people to carry out their vision.

Putting on the Whole Armor

Ephesians 6:11
Put on the full armor of God so that you can take your stand against the devil's schemes.

What are some of the other tools a leader needs? Here are twenty qualities a leader must have to be effective:

Optimism—Once you discover your purpose, you have a positive attitude.

Energy—All of a sudden, you will have lots of energy to put into it. You can work nearly nonstop.

Warmth—You realize that everybody is important. God made each in His image. You love everybody and treat all with warm regard.

Integrity—You can be true to yourself and conduct all of your affairs with integrity.

Trustworthiness—Integrity leads others to trust you. You must earn trust by being worthy of it.

Responsibility—True leaders do not stop until the job is finished. They never make excuses. They may give reasons but not excuses.

Self-Image—Leaders do not need outside confirmation of their worth. They know who they are and what they have to do.

Knowledge—Leaders have an insatiable appetite for knowledge, constantly expanding their minds. A leader is a reader. A leader pursues wisdom.

Submission—Leaders must be followers too when necessary. They must submit to the will of God, to higher authorities, to those with greater knowledge of a subject, to those with a different area of gifting and often to the will of the people. If your car is broken down, you must submit to the mechanic.

Self-Discipline—Discipline involves meeting standards for a greater purpose. Self-discipline calls for self-imposed standards of excellence for a greater purpose. It calls for behavior change, denying yourself certain things to achieve something else. The word Jesus uses for His followers is "disciples."

Morality — A leader cannot be effective if they have moral failings. It saps energy and destroys purpose. A leader does not have time to let personal or marital problems detract from the mission. Keep your house in order.

Friendliness — A leader has to have people skills and must make people feel drawn to him. It is difficult to lead people who are angry with you or who just do not like you. You must be personable, and likewise you have to like people. As a leader, you cannot always be everybody's friend, but you can be friendly, friend-like.

Humor — To be an effective leader you have to laugh at life and not take it too seriously. Humor helps win people over to your point of view. Laugh at yourself and have fun. Be able to laugh at mistakes, yours and others'. Laugh at things that you cannot control anyway. Be able to laugh in the midst of crisis.

Resilience — A leader has to be able to bounce back from a fall or a catastrophe. Deal with it and get back in there.

Experience — A leader has a track record for success. A leader comes with a history. The problems you are going through right now are qualifying you for leadership. Do not rush through them. Learn as you go, because God is preparing you. He is not finished with you yet. It is on-the-job training for greatness.

Creativity — Leaders know more than one way to solve a problem. Leaders are always suspicious of those who say, "This is the way" or "We have never done it that way" or even "It has to be done *my* way." A leader has the ability to walk around a problem and see it from twenty different angles. A leader loves new approaches, suggestions, and ideas, even when they are not her own.

Flexibility — Leaders are not afraid to change. They know how to adapt and can make adjustments for other people's opinions, needs, or comfort. Adjusting to others or to a situation is not a weakness.

Humility — A true leader does not care who gets the credit. Leaders are more concerned about results than about awards, recognition, praise, or even thanks for what they do.

Courage—A leader must be willing to take risks, to act on instinct, and to act alone when no one else will help. The leader also must be willing to do right when no one else does, and to make the call when no one else will make a decision.

Concepts—Leaders see the big picture and do not let details overwhelm them. Leaders have a sense of being able to see concepts that no one else can see. They can look at a situation and see the relationships between the parts, like the parts of a car: how the terminal wire relates to the battery, the battery to the engine, and the engine to the mission of travel.

A Leadership Tools Inventory

Different leaders will be stronger on one quality than on another. Some can make up for what they lack on one point by being strong on another, but all leaders should have some degree of strength in most, if not all, of them. If you are lacking on any one quality, work on it. Integrity, trustworthiness, morality, and self-discipline especially must seem obvious, but we have had so many recent scandals in public life, we must be vigilant in our own leadership and selecting whom we will follow.

All of the qualities—along with the essential tools of purpose, passion, conviction, and inspiration—will help you to be a leader in your designated, prepared spot, located in your area of gifting, serving it to the world.

To determine if you are ready to fulfill your assignment, ask yourself:

Can I inspire people?
Do I know my purpose?
What is my passion?
How do I show conviction?
Do I have integrity?
Am I trustworthy?
Do I take risks and welcome the unknown?
Do I have the other qualities of a leader?
Am I willing to work on those in which I am weak?

The Benefits of Servant Leadership

When you discover your purpose, you can tap into your authority to fulfill your leadership role. You may begin to wonder what is in it for you. "What do I get out of it? When can I begin to enjoy some of the benefits of the job?" When our earthly jobs provide things like health insurance, pensions, and paid vacation time, we call those benefits. The perks of a leadership assignment are somewhat different, and they become part of the arsenal you need to carry out the mission.

Here are some of the benefits servant leadership provides to you and to those you serve:

Authenticity/Authority

True servant leaders exercise inherent authority to do what they were born to do and fulfill their purpose.

When you discover your gift, you find your arena of authority in this world. Authority is the inherent ability not only to execute your gift but also to do what you were born to do. If you are not doing that, you are working against your own authority and doing something your Maker did not design you to do.

A bird that is flying is authentic because it is doing what the Creator designed it to do. The Creator designed and authorized the bird to fly.

After Jesus' resurrection, He appeared to His students (who were about to graduate from leadership school and become fellow workers with Him) and said that since He had been given "all authority" by the Creator-Father, He was giving them authority to go train other students who would learn to be coworkers as well.

Matthew 28:18–20
18 "All authority in heaven and on earth has been given to me.
19 Therefore go and make disciples of all nations…
20 and teaching them to obey everything I have commanded you. And surely I am with you always, to the very end of the age."

When you discover who you are, and are able to live it out, you can be authentic. There are many "unauthorized dealers" in this world. They are doing things they were not born to do. The reason they have to work so hard is that they do not have any authority in that area. A fish is authorized to swim, so swimming is easy for it. Yet, if a fish leaped off a steep cliff and tried to fly, it would die. Unauthentic leadership requires high maintenance. It is hard work maintaining something not meant to be.

This is why you must find your gift, start working on it, and let it grow. When your gift kicks in, everything you need to sustain it already exists.

Luke 12:24, 27–28
24 Consider the ravens: They do not sow or reap, they have no storeroom or barn; yet God feeds them. And how much more valuable you are than birds!...
27 Consider how the lilies grow. They do not labor or spin. Yet I tell you, not even Solomon in all his splendor was dressed like one of these.
28 If that is how God clothes the grass of the field, which is here today, and tomorrow is thrown into the fire, how much more will he clothe you, O you of little faith!

The flowers do not feel stress. They do not toil. They are not concerned about paying rent and mortgages, or feeding kids and affording tuition. They are not trying to do anything but just be flowers, and God has clothed them brilliantly for that. The birds and the fish have everything they need to fulfill their purpose. The Creator wants you to be yourself and fulfill your purpose. When you do, the Creator supplies everything you need.

Two Birds

One day on my way to Australia to speak at a leadership conference, I had a brief layover in Atlanta, Georgia. As I sat near the window watching the aircrafts land, suddenly I was attracted to the arrival of another bird of flight, a seagull. Standing there spellbound, I realized I was watching two birds at work—one naturally born to fly, the other a fabricated imitation.

One bird is authentic, the other unnatural. One is original, the other a copy. One with natural authority, the other with unnatural authority.

The seagull, gliding on the natural currents of the wind, gently landed right in front of the massive aircraft that arrived to take me to my next destination. Suddenly, over two dozen men and women went into action with machines, hoses, blocks, guiding lights, generators, and all sorts of equipment to service the big bird that approached the jet bridge.

No one moved toward the sea gull.

One of the men ran to the front of the big bird, two to the side, one grabbed an air-conditioning hose; another was in a fuel truck, another in a catering van, and still another drove a conveyer belt vehicle; there were baggage handlers, mechanics, engineers, and cabin cleaners. No one moved toward the seagull. The natural bird needed no one to service him. He needed no artificial oxygen supply, catering, cleaning, fuel, and the like. It was amazing.

In that moment, I learned one of the most important lessons in life: when you are natural and do what you were naturally created to do, then maintenance is low. If you try to do something you were not naturally born to do, then you will need high maintenance and depend on artificial sustenance. The cost of upkeep will be extreme.

There at the window at the airport I learned again the power of discovering your natural area of gifting and dedicating yourself to developing, refining, and exercising your gift. If you attempt to do something you were not created or designed to do by your Creator, then you will spend most of your life on maintenance and not in service. Life becomes a struggle, a torture, and a burden.

The bird is a leader in the area of flight and does it without heavy maintenance. When you find your spot and exercise your gift in service to the world, your leadership becomes natural and effortless.

Originality
True servant leaders are not copies but originals.

Until you discover your gift, you can only be an imitation. When you discover who you are, you become an original; you are no longer a copy. As a leader, you are unique. Leaders are self-contained. By this,

I mean they do not get the meaning of their lives from other people. They are originals. Servant leadership is born when people discover their authentic selves and naturally become one of a kind.

Genuine Confidence
True servant leaders possess a natural confidence, emanating from a sense of self-knowledge, produced by an awareness of their true value and potential in the world.

When you find your gift, you also find your confidence. That confidence is not a cover-up for feeling inadequate; it is genuine. As you exercise your natural abilities, you find you do not need to try to impress others anymore. You do not need to brag. You are who you are, focusing on your purpose, not on building your ego.

What usually makes a person lack confidence is incompetence. When you have a good command of the execution of something, then confidence is natural. Those who are insecure in themselves will sometimes interpret that confidence in you as arrogance or pride, when, in fact, it is the ultimate expression of humility because you are not trying to be something you are not; you are being yourself. By understanding and moving forward with your purpose, you can know exactly who you are and be confident that you can fulfill it using your inherent gifts.

Personal Fulfillment
True servant leaders find fulfillment in serving their gift to others, not for a price but for pleasure and fulfillment.

Once you are pursuing your purpose and using your gifts, you experience what is foreign to so many people: fulfillment. Suddenly you have joy, peace, and satisfaction because you are doing what you were born to do. You are fulfilled because using your gift is its own reward for you. You are filled with purpose. You have taken charge of your leadership spot.

How much luckier can you be than to spend your time doing something that pleases you and pleases God? You are pleased because you can use your area of gifting, and God is pleased because you are carrying out His assignment. Other people are pleased because you are helping them fulfill their assignments. If you help other people get what they need, you will always have what you need.

Intrinsic Value
True servant leaders derive their self-worth from their conscious conviction that they are important to the world and are obligated to contribute to humankind.

When you discover who you are, you understand your value to the world and your importance to the human race. You recognize you have a contribution to make.

What is important here is that your value does not come from the world. Rather, you give your value to the world. Your value comes from the recognition that you can supply something no one else on earth has. That is your significance.

When you know who you are, you do not need to impress anyone. You do not have to prove anything to anybody. You can just be yourself and understand your value to the world.

No Competition
True servant leaders never compete or strive with other leaders but find pleasure in the success of others and contribute their gift to the success of others.

When you discover who you are, there is no one to compete with because you are an original. Other people's gifts or successes do not threaten you because you know that others can never replace or become you. You cannot take my place, and I cannot take yours, so the competition is over. Building on our earlier analogy, the battery does not need to compete with the spark plug, because the battery can never fulfill the function of the spark plug, and vice versa. They all need to sit in their spots and serve the engine with their individual gifts.

No Comparison
True servant leaders compliment, not compare, themselves with others. Their sense of values gives them a sense of security that allows them to never be threatened by the success of others.

When you discover who you are, you become distinctive. If you are a true servant leader, you do not compare yourself to anyone else because you know there is no one like you. Measuring yourself and your gifts against other people becomes a non-issue.

It is counter productive to compare a battery with a spark plug to try to decide which is better; both are unique and needed. Likewise, you cannot compare two servant-leader business executives, teachers, store owners, veterinarians, artists, beauticians, journalists, or economists. Each has a place, and none is inferior or excluded.

Two servant leaders in the same field can actually help each other succeed, because they cannot damage each other's success. However, people who are not sure who they are remain insecure and grasping. They are constantly comparing such things as the relative size of businesses, attendance, academic degrees, income, and even looks.

Yet what do some businesses do? They have so much confidence in the uniqueness of what they have to offer that they will build right down the street from a business that sells to a similar consumer. McDonald's and Burger King do this. Lowe's and Home Depot do the same. Each has unique products and services that allow them to do this.

Instead of comparing yourself to others, servant leadership allows you to develop your own gifts and strengths to their fullest capacity.

No Jealousy
True servant leaders rejoice in the progress and the success of others. Servant leaders understand and value the gift and contribution others bring to their lives.

Servant leadership naturally eliminates jealousy, because when you discover your authenticity, you know you are one of a kind. You cannot be me, and I cannot be you; we can never be threats to one another. Your spot belongs to you, and my spot belongs to me.

Jealousy is only possible when you believe that someone can take away what you have, or that someone has something you do not have. Servant leadership cancels that because no one can take away your purpose and gifts. You have infinite value through your unique contribution to the world.

No Fear

True servant leadership expresses a calm security and confidence that is a by-product of convictions that the leader is unique and irreplaceable to the world. Fear is the manifestation of insecurity, low self-esteem, and a lack of personal vision and a sense of purpose.

Servant leadership also eliminates feelings of fear. You do not have to be alarmed or suspicious of anyone else's actions. Your belief about and in yourself, based on who you are and what you have been given to do, cancels out the fear of others undermining you.

The Master said, "If you love Me, keep My commandments" (*John 14:15* nkjv). He did not say, "If you fear me…" We cannot love what we fear. The condition for doing what this Leader asks is love, not coercion. Most insecure leaders present God as a tyrant in order to get you to fear them. Jesus of Nazareth taught that the Creator is our Father and we should worry for nothing, like lilies of the field. The Creator is a good Father, not someone who desires to destroy us. Likewise, we are not to cultivate fear to manipulate others.

Internal Motivation and Passion

True servant leaders are motivated from within by their passion and purpose.

When you discover your gift and its corresponding areas of authority and authenticity, you no longer need external motivation or prodding. You recognize your assignment. You discover what you are supposed to provide to the world, and you can get busy. This will motivate you for the rest of your life. Your passion gets you up in the morning, fills you with energy throughout the day, and keeps you looking ahead to the future with confidence.

These constitute the toolbox of the servant leader. Are you ready to begin putting the tools to work? First, you have a little more work to do as you refine your gifts.

14

Refine: Be a Limited Edition

"The key to success is discovering your uniqueness and significance."

L et us say you want to open a shoe store, but your city already has one thousand of them. How do you get people to come to yours? The first question you should address is how your area of gifting applies in this realm. "Where is my leadership spot?"

You have a natural-born gift for selling, and you already have experience in shoe sales at the retail and wholesale levels. Now, you have to refine your idea and make your shop unique. You decide: "I will only sell shoes for babies and toddlers, children under 2 years old, because I do that well, I love small children, there are many young families in this area, and I know no one else is specializing in baby shoes."

That will make your store unique. You have done your business plan, studied the market, and advertised your specialty. You have set fair prices and stocked a broad selection. You decide to sell at retail in a brick-and-mortar store, as well as worldwide on the Internet.

Whenever people want baby shoes, the first place they think of will be your store. They will drive across town to take advantage of your selection, prices, and expertise. They will go to your e-commerce site on the Worldwide Web and buy baby shoes in multiples. They will tell their friends. You are fulfilling a specific need—serving your gift, your specialty, your uniqueness, your knowledge of shoes for the infant-to-toddler market. It is not a coincidence that you are dominating the market and making a handsome profit.

Each of us makes ourselves valuable to the world by identifying a gift so unique that no one can find our skills and contributions anywhere else.

Go to a discount store and look at the racks of clothes. Dozens of shirts, slacks, and dresses fill the racks, but they all look alike. That is why they are so inexpensive. The store makes its profit off the volume of sales. Next, visit the finest jewelry store in town, and you are likely to see only one of each gemstone on display. Each stone may be the only one of its kind in the world known to exist, and the stonecutter has taken care to shape and polish it in a way that will bring out its rare brilliance. Uniqueness makes things valuable. Similarly, when you learn to reflect your one-of-a-kind gift, you will be valuable to the world.

Being different—rare, one-of-a-kind, exclusive, a limited edition—makes things expensive and desirable.

Even gold has little use in its raw form. It requires a process of *refinement* to expose its beauty and purity. As valuable as oil is, it too must be refined from a crude form to make it useful to us. Likewise, we must refine our gifts to make them valuable so that we can serve them to others most effectively and successfully.

Refine has several meanings. It means to be free from impurities, imperfections, or coarseness. It can mean to remove *moral imperfection* or to improve by introducing *subtleties or distinctions.*

Value + Refinement = Success

Someone asked me, "What is the key to success?" I said, "If you want to be successful, first of all, stop seeking success." Value plus refinement equals success. Success is becoming a person of value. Stop trying to be successful; seek to be a person of value. Make yourself valuable to the world.

You become valuable by making yourself so unique that people cannot find anything like you or your product anywhere else. Your uniqueness makes you valuable. When you make yourself valuable, people will come to you for your gift. You need not pursue success. Success will result from your value to others. You succeed by helping others achieve their mission and fulfill their needs.

Value is the key to servant leadership.
Value is determined by refined uniqueness.
Success is becoming a person of value.

An Unexpected Visitor

Les Brown is a well-known motivational speaker and author in the United States. He had read my books and had been using some of my materials. When he came to the Bahamas several years ago, he asked a taxi driver, "Do you know Dr. Myles Munroe?"

The driver said, "Yes."

Brown said, "Take me to his house."

Because our island is so small, everybody knows where everyone lives. The taxicab brought him to my house. My housekeeper called me at my office to say there was a guy in my house who wanted to meet me. His name was Les Brown.

"Who is Les Brown?" I thought, and then I said, "Put him on the phone."

This man was in my house talking to me on my own telephone. He said, "I am Les Brown," and he explained who he was.

I said, "Oh yeah, I think I do know you. What are you doing in my house?" He told me of his interest in my work.

I hurried home, and we sat together the entire afternoon. He asked me a whole lot of questions—questions about my writings and about my concepts of human value. How did I get to understand principles that he thought were very profound? He wanted to know my secret to understanding these things. I shared my convictions with him, and we have become very good friends, even working or appearing together on occasion—always trying to improve the lot of our fellow humans.

Les Brown was already famous in his own right. He could have figured out what I shared with him some other way. Yet, he went out of his way to find me, because he was that determined to *refine* his own message.

When you know your *purpose*, you will seek out others who can help you. You will go a great distance to find them. You will try to learn what others have to say about the thing you do. You will read everything you can get your hands on about it. You will never accept that you already know all there is to know about it. Those who have found their spot and are serving their gift continue to refine.

Putting a Value on You

The pursuit of *success* is in our psyche, especially in the fields of business and government. Yet success in leadership—for anyone, in any area of life—is contingent upon a sense of personal value to the world.

We often have a hard time understanding the concept of personal value. If another person deserves our respect and honor, this does not mean he or she is superior to us. Many of our societies promote the personality cult—idolizing celebrities in entertainment, sports, business, and even religion. The Internet is even helping to create instant celebrities of people we never heard of the day before. We hear endless humiliating gossip, self-serving publicity, and intimate details about people who are often famous just for being famous, not for great talent. Our children even spend countless hours trying to look, sound, or live like these celebrities.

Idolizing or worshiping another human being is a sign that you do not believe you are very valuable. To be a servant leader, you must understand that no other human being on the planet is more—or less—valuable than you are. If anyone suggests he or she is more valuable than you are, my recommendation is that you avoid that person.

The greatest discovery in human experience is self-discovery, because with it comes an understanding of our origin in the Creator, our inherent value, and the manner in which we are to fulfill our personal leadership purpose. Personal leadership is the divine assignment for which God designed and made you. Your leadership attitude will come alive when you discover and start living according to your true nature.

When you discover who you really are, people's opinions of you suddenly fall to the ground. I have discovered that the greatest deliverance in the world is not deliverance from evil spirits, but from other people. An attitude of freedom and confidence is a by-product of our self-discovery.

True servant leaders have a sense of divine obligation to the betterment of mankind. They believe they owe a debt to their generation and are committed to pay it. But you cannot help people when you still need their approval. You have to be free from them first; then you can help them.

The only way to discover yourself is to discover the Creator. You and your Creator are of the same nature. Your life on earth will make no sense if you do not know yourself. And only the Creator truly knows you, because no one knows a product like its manufacturer. Since only your Creator knows why He made you, you have to go to Him to discover your true self.

True leadership is more discovery of self than a position to attain.

Personal leadership is not a matter of *employment* but of *deployment*. It is to deploy yourself in your generation for the benefit of all generations. An employer should hire people with the understanding that he is providing an opportunity for them to deploy their gifts, making them better and greater. A job is an opportunity to be paid to refine and deploy your gift in the interest of serving the vision and mission of your organization.

The key is in *knowing* that you have a contribution to make to the world that no one else can make, that the Creator has bestowed you with a gift to give to humanity that no one else can give. Jesus knew, for example, that He came to earth to be the ransom for humanity. That

made Him of ultimate importance to the human race. He stressed His
purpose many times:

Luke 19:10
For the Son of Man came to seek and to save what was lost.

Matthew 20:28
The Son of Man did not come to be served, but to serve, and to give his life as a ran-
som for many.

The world desperately needed him. His knowledge of his significance made him a confident servant of the Creator–Father. He knew he
had to reveal his gift to the world.

Get an Attitude

Personal leadership success depends on an attitude of servant leadership that comes from understanding our value to others. Peter,
one of Jesus' leadership graduates, thoroughly understood this. He
wrote, "Be shepherds of God's flock that is under your care, serving as
overseers—not because you must, but because you are willing, as God
wants you to be; not greedy for money, but eager to serve; not Lording
it over those entrusted to you, but being examples to the flock" (*1 Peter*
5:2–3).

It is only when we are convinced of our value to the world that we
are able to serve others willingly, eagerly, faithfully, and with integrity. Along with such an attitude of service, the *qualities* of personal
servant leadership must be manifest in a leader's life. These qualities
are qualities of our Creator. The first–century theologian Paul wrote a
letter to the Creator's servant leaders in the Roman province of Gala-
tia and listed them. "The fruit of the Spirit is love, joy, peace, patience,
kindness, goodness, faithfulness, gentleness and self–control" (*Galatians*
5:22–23).

Servant leadership does not make demands on people or treat them harshly. Instead, it serves the world with these qualities or fruit of the Spirit.

Perceived Value

The key to leading others is that they perceive your gift as significant. You are significant if you have refined and developed your gift to the point that others will want it and know they can receive it only if they come to you. They will see that you are the only one who can meet that specific need. Whether you have goods or a service to offer, you must demonstrate that it has been refined and is unique.

When you want a Big Mac, you cannot go to Burger King; and when you want a Whopper, you cannot go to McDonald's. Both are billion-dollar companies, and both sell sandwiches. They are both successful because they have refined their sandwiches. They have it down to a science. You cannot exactly reproduce these sandwiches or make them in your own house. These companies have refined their product and become significant to consumers.

Likewise, every human being comes equipped with a unique gift that has value, that makes him or her significant to the world. This is equally true whether you have just graduated from high school, or are 50 years old and hold a Ph.D. If you want to be a great leader, find your gift and serve it to the world.

As I have noted, education alone cannot give you a gift; it can help you refine a gift. Many of us waste time studying things that have no relationship to our area of gifting. Many have earned degrees in something they hate. We do this because our parents, teachers, preachers, or counselors advise us that we will make more money or have a more secure future if we study what they say is the up-and-coming thing.

"I know you want to act, but get a teaching certificate—just in case."

"I know you want to write poetry, but why don't you get a degree in accounting—just to fall back on."

"You might not make it as an artist. Why don't you get a nursing degree or go to secretarial school?"

A parent may tell his or her child, "I'm paying for your tuition, so you have to study this instead." As a parent, you may not realize what the Creator has given to your child. Cultivate his or her interests. Observe your child's passion and encourage it. Young people should not study what their guidance counselors or parents tell them to study in college, even if it is "one of the fastest-growing fields." They should study the subject that is their passion.

Do not get a degree in something you hate. Your degree may kill you. The work it leads to will give you tension, stress, and high blood pressure. That is like paying for a degree in sickness.

For the same reasons, people should not just seek jobs but seek their purpose. You must find your passion and study it.

Remember these points:

Do not work for money.
Work for fulfillment.
Financial success will follow.

The secret of servant leadership is that your leadership is in your gift of value. Remember Solomon's wisdom: "A man's gift makes room for him, and brings him before great men" (*Proverbs 18:16* nkjv). He did not say one's education or even connections make room for him in the world, but rather man's *gift*. When you refine your gift and really work on it until it becomes significant, the world will make room for you.

Opportunity Finds You

Ron Kenoly, a well-known singer and recording artist, told me that for seventeen years he served as a worship leader at a church on the West Coast. He said he worked hard, developing musicians and writing music. A man came to the church one day and stood in the back. He listened to Ron, and he heard the worship team. After the service, he came up and greeted the pastor.

The pastor said, "Who are you?"

The man said he was president of a record label. "I'm in the area," he said. "I came to visit your church. Who's that guy?" he asked, looking at Ron Kenoly. What he could have said was, "Who's that diamond?"

Ron told me that he had been so busy having fun in serving his gift in the local church that he never thought of greatness. He was serving his gift to the worshipers.

The pastor called him over and introduced him to the visitor, who said, "I'd like to talk with you for a few minutes, you and your pastor." They went back in the office and talked.

Kenoly said that within five minutes, the stranger said, "I'll offer you a recording deal. We'd like you to come in, please bring all of your equipment, and record a live concert. We want to put you on our label."

Ron's first album, *Jesus Is Alive*, was recorded live at his Jubilee Christian Center church in San Jose, California, in 1991 by Integrity/Hosanna records [Wikipedia], and he has recorded more than a half dozen successful gospel albums since then. He now heads Ron Kenoly Ministries International and the Academy of Praise, based in Orlando, Florida.

My own career got a similar boost from a chance occurrence—a divine opportunity. I was in a 10×10 foot office in a shopping center when I received a phone call. Someone asked me to speak for one evening at a conference because the main speaker could not be there. I said, "Sure."

I was used to speaking to two hundred people. When I arrived at the meeting, I learned fifteen thousand were attending! I spoke, never looking at one note, because what I was teaching I had refined for fifteen years. A television network showed up, and I have been on television ever since. Your gift makes room for you when you serve yourself to the world.

The better you become at your gift, at serving your gift, the more people are attracted to you. True leaders do not seek followers. Followers seek leaders. And most important, leaders seek other leaders who can serve them in their special area of gifting. That is where that magnetic combination comes into play. Jesus maximized His gifts so effectively that the people came looking for the gift. Followers do not really follow leaders; they seek the gift being served.

When your gift becomes refined, those in need of it will look for

you, and they will pay you to give of yourself. People will come looking for you to eat from your tree, and they will even pay for the fruit.
Your prosperity is in your gift, not in your salary.

"What do you do when you have more than one gift?" Develop all
of them but maximize one of them. Be mindful of the old saying "jack
of all trades, master of none." Never abandon any of your gifts, but
master at least one. And use your gifts in cooperation with each other,
while you focus on one. Your primary gift becomes your significant
contribution. I spent a lot of my life developing my musical gifts, and I
studied art. I still use my music, and I sometimes paint for friends, but
I have maximized my gifts of communicating to focus on the mission
of developing leaders.

The Right Environment

Part of the process of refining your gift might be deciding whether
your present circumstances allow you to find out who you really are.
Can you develop your leadership where you are?

Suppose I put an apple seed on a windowsill and leave it there for
fifty years. What happens? Nothing. Is an apple tree in that seed? Yes,
but you have to move from the windowsill and get into the soil of pos-
sibilities. Make a decision now that you are going to manifest yourself
to the world. You will bless the world with your fruit and bring forth
the Creator's blessing.

Getting into the right atmosphere and environment is very important. A bird cannot fly if you lock it away in your house in a 2×2 foot
cage—something like your job. You are capable of doing some great
things, but your job traps you in a cubicle that is maybe 5×5 feet if
you are lucky. You are just like a caged bird, or a fish in a bowl. God
did not design the fish to be in your house in a little bowl so you can
watch it, or even in a large aquarium. The Creator designed fish to be in
the ocean, to enjoy the unlimited vastness of the sea. We trap ash in a
container as some jobs trap people.

You may have even trapped yourself in a marriage. That is why
the Bible says, "Marriage should be honored by all" (*Hebrews 13:4*). The

word *honored* means to be "esteemed highly, highly respected," and to be "considered with sober judgment." You can dream as big as you want, go as far as you want, but if you marry the wrong person, your home can become like a birdcage.

Before you get married, talk to the perspective lucky person and say to him or her, "Before we proceed any further, can I please advise you of how high I plan to fly—just in case you have any ideas of building a cage around my life? I am an eagle. If you're a pigeon, go somewhere else." If you are an eagle, do not marry a pigeon. Pigeons cannot fly where eagles fly.

Perhaps your parents are opposed to your career plans. While you have to respect them, you also have to live your life. You know your heart and your gift. If it is right for you, they will have to learn to live with it. You have to conduct the Father's business. Now, you might have to leave their home and do without their support to get into the right environment, but you have to do what you have to do. It is important that you be true to yourself and pursue your personal vision and passion because this will be your only source of fulfillment. This passion is your context of contribution to humanity. Whatever you were created to do, the Creator is obligated to supply the provisions for your assignment, so be persistent.

Maybe you will need many years of schooling to make the best use of your gift. Your gift might be music. You are naturally gifted. You have perfect pitch. You play by ear and sing like a nightingale, but to use this gift effectively, to perform at a professional level, to compose music others can reproduce, or to teach people in church or in a college, you will need to study music formally. You have to get into the right music school or apprentice with the right voice coach. You might have to get experience with several orchestras or travel to Europe to study in the right opera houses. You have to get into the right environment to manifest the gift. Even if you want to specialize, you will still need to broaden your horizons. You might have to learn classical music and bluegrass banjo, even if you plan to spend your life directing and playing for a gospel choir. Similarly, if you are planning to devote your life to classical music, you will probably be required to have an understanding of folk music, African American spirituals, jazz, and the blues.

You are carrying your future like a pregnancy. You must develop; you have to go through your nine months; perhaps you experience some morning sickness and discomfort. If you cannot persevere through the morning sickness, you will not get to enjoy the laughter of the baby. When my wife was pregnant, she would say, "I feel so bad." But you cannot quit because you feel bad. You do not quit because the baby is taking too long to come. You have to go through the process to birth your refined leadership gift.

Like a pregnant woman who has to get different clothes eventually, because she has outgrown her regular clothes, you might have to shed some people. Some who started out with you before the pregnancy cannot stand to be around you when you are big. Sometimes you need different people around you. You need midwives, not critics. Some people are with you at the conception but cannot handle growth. The birthing process is not easy.

Action Steps

You have a lot of work to do before you can make the most of your leadership spot. How are you going to get into position?

First, you must set aside time for quiet reading, prayer, meditation, and study. Make it a project. That is how you discover yourself and begin to discern your Creator's purpose. You cannot lead if you cannot hear God's will for you and if you cannot hear yourself think.

Your leadership attitude, the leadership spirit, will come alive when you discover and start living according to your true nature. You and the Father are one, because you are the very image of God. The only way to discover you is to discover God.

To prepare to lead, you must:

Spend time alone in thought
Write down your desires and visions
Read books on leadership and other topics

Identify people who can help you

Take advantage of opportunities to learn

Develop a plan to fulfill your purpose

Prepare to carry it out

Volunteer your services

These steps are a necessary part of refining your gift because:

The Creator will reveal your purpose only if you have a passion to know it. If you have no desire to discover your gifting, you will probably never find it.

The Creator will only tell you what you want to know. If you do not desire information, He will not force it on you. I have come to believe that God only gives information on a desire-to-know basis.

The Creator will only show you what you want to see. If you do not want to have a vision for your life, you will not get one.

The Creator will only take you as far as you want to go. If you do not want to go any further, you will stay wherever you are.

One of the ways these concepts have been proven to me is not only by experience but also by statements the Creator Himself makes. "You will seek me and find me when you seek me with all your heart" (Jeremiah 29:13). Many people think that because God is everywhere, He is always easy to "find." It is not so. We have to be serious about seeking Him. We cannot just seek Him casually, but must search with all our hearts.

How badly do you want to know your purpose? This is what the Creator is always checking. This is why most of the Pharisees could never understand Jesus. They had decided they knew enough. They did not want to know more about Him than their presuppositions led them to think. They were those the prophet Isaiah spoke about: "You will be ever hearing but never understanding; you will be ever seeing but never perceiving. For this people's heart has become calloused; they hardly hear with their ears, and they have closed their *eyes*" (*Matthew 13:14–15*).

Do you really desire to know your purpose? Tell the Creator you want to know more. He will open your mind.

You need to spend time with the Manufacturer and say, "Introduce me to myself again." You need to receive the original vision He had for your life. Take everything you thought you were and give it to Him. Let Him show you something you never saw before.

The Vision Statement

By reading this book, you have already begun the process of learning to see what you never saw before—of refining your purpose and finding your leadership spot. Now you are ready to begin writing down your dreams and putting your purpose on paper. To define your leadership edge and refine your uniqueness, try this mission statement or "vision statement" exercise:

Write the answers to these questions:

My purpose: Why do I exist? What is God's plan for me?

My vision: What is the end or result I can foresee?

My goals: What do I plan to do? What do I want to do? How can I make it unique?

My objectives: Why am I doing this? What are my reasons and motivations?

My plan: How will I do it? With whom? When? Where?

My strategy: How can I refine it? How long will it take? What is my timetable? What resources will I need?

Some answers will be more important than others will, depending on your specific leadership spot. Redraft your answers into a short mission statement or "leadership statement." Take your time to rewrite and *refine* it as often as necessary until you can state it in one or two paragraphs, or eventually a sentence.

In Christ's example: "I came to serve and to give my life as a ransom for many" (see *Matthew 20:28*).

I might express mine like this: "I teach servant leadership principles to help people find and refine their leadership spot and serve their gifts to benefit humanity and help create the world God intended."

Someone else's might be, "I live for golf. I am good at it and I play it professionally to give others pleasure."

"I tell jokes to make people laugh and forget their troubles for a few minutes."

"I specialize in selling shoes for the newborn-to-toddler market in stores and on the Internet to corner that market, make a profit, and be a service to young families."

"I teach the principles of nonviolence to free my people and heal a nation."

Keep your statement where you can see it and refer to it often. It is a foundation for your leadership assignment.

Now you are ready to explore your vision.

15

Envision: Order My Steps

"The greatest Gift given to mankind is the gift of Vision not sight."

How do you know that the vision you have for your life is from God? How do you distinguish between personal ambition and divine vision?

The answer to those questions is simple: if your vision improves only your life, focuses only on your needs, and fulfills only your private dreams, it is *not* a divine vision. Any true vision, motivated by the Creator, will improve the lives of those around you. Servant leadership is about the others. It is not about us. Servant leadership is becoming yourself for the advantage of others. True vision will always benefit and improve others, never harm or destroy them.

True vision does not exist to benefit the visionary, as the car does not exist to get itself around. Your vision might be to have a big house, but that is not a vision from God—unless He wants you to have it so you can fill it up with children orphaned by AIDS or the homeless. If your vision is to have a big car, that is not a vision from God—unless He wants you to have it to transport the needy, the infirmed, and the elderly to get medical help. Your desire for the big house or the big car is ambition, not vision. A truly authentic vision will always serve humanity to make it better. *It will always advance humanity, develop people, benefit people.* If so, it is probably a vision from God.

Selling drugs is not a vision from God. Stealing property is not a vision from God. A vision from God will always benefit other people.

A woman told me not long ago, "My passion is to become a model." I asked, "OK, why?" When she could not answer, I said, "Then, that is not God's call for your life. If you can't tell me how it's going to benefit humanity, you had better go check God again."

Vision flows from your purpose. Purpose is why you were born. Vision comes when you see your purpose. When you can feel your purpose, you can see your vision.

For example, you may have a passion that comes from your desire to help children. You just love children. It makes you angry to see them hurting. That is a sign: whatever makes you angry probably is tied to your purpose.

Whenever you say, "Someone has to fix that…someone should do something about that," God is revealing your purpose. You are that someone. You feel this thing for kids. You cannot figure out what it is. You do not know why, but you just hate to see kids who are abused, wayward, and lost. It really eats you up. The person next to you is not moved by it, but seeing children suffer can make you cry. You do not even know the children. When you see visions of how you can make changes, when you begin to see pictures in your mind of what you can do about it, you are moving into vision.

Having a wider field of vision in your area of gifting than others do is part of your gift as a leader. When you serve your vision to others, they benefit. You were born with a vision, and your passion in life is to bring that vision out for the benefit of humanity. When you become a passionate visionary for the benefit of others, you are a leader.

In matters pertaining to your area of gifting, I will follow you because you have shown me a picture of the world, as you see it. It is a vision worthy of my cooperation with you. You have made me see the value of working with you or through you to fulfill this picture you painted. I can see where you are taking me.

Recall that in Chapter 13, we learned:

Passion is motivated by a vision, birthed from a conviction, and produced by a sense of purpose.

Vision is purpose in pictures. Vision is conviction in Technicolor. Vision is the capacity to see beyond what your eyes take in.

True leadership is the manifestation of passion generated by a vision that regulates the priority and energy of a leader. The leader possesses the vision. Then the vision possesses the leader. All true visionary leaders possess a sense of destiny.

It is my conviction that leadership without vision is simply management. While the transition from manager to leader may be a natural progression, it is not an automatic promotion. In general, leaders were previously managers, but not all managers will become leaders. Managers maintain well, organize well. Leaders have vision. They make things happen. To visionary leaders, the vision is their reality and is the purpose for their leadership. It is vision that provides the momentum for leadership, and it is the end for which leadership exists. It is vision that gives meaning to leadership. Vision is the heart of leadership and is the measure of effective leadership. Vision is the inspiration of leadership. Vision gives legitimacy to leadership as it gives followers the noble justification for submitting their energies, talents, resources, and dedication to a cause. Vision provides the direction and force for leadership. Leadership begins and ends with *vision*.

Conveying the Vision

However, the most important practical role of true leadership is to communicate the vision. Leaders effectively transfer ownership of the vision. True leaders train others to fulfill the vision; they think generationally. The goal of communicating the vision to others is to blend and submit everyone's personal visions in the corporate vision.

Communication in leadership is like blood to the body. Vision should be reduced to one sentence if it is to be communicated and executed effectively. Without communication, leadership cannot be successful. The leader must share his or her passion with infectious self-confidence, vitality, energy, and personal dynamism.

The leader must express feelings for the vision assertively, using animated facial and physical expressions to manifest the passion. Communication must be optimistic. By communicating the vision, the leader inspires people, giving them a broader purpose than their immediate jobs, providing energy, excitement, and direction. The leader must communicate the vision in such a way that others take ownership of it. The vision itself should be concise; be easily remembered; represent a future better than the present; reflect the values and aspirations of the people; and transcend the daily activities of life. The vision should uplift and inspire others to believe in the future.

The purest form of leadership is influence through inspiration. Inspiration is the opposite of intimidation and absent of manipulation. It comes from the divine deposit of destiny in the hearts of men and women who have a vision of the purpose for which the Creator made them.

To summarize: practical leadership is the capacity to influence, inspire, rally, direct, encourage, motivate, induce, move, mobilize, and activate others to pursue a common goal or purpose, while maintaining commitment, momentum, confidence, and courage.

Write It Down: Documented Purpose

What is vision?

Vision is the product of purpose.
Vision is the source of true leadership.
Vision is documented purpose.

You cannot say you have a vision if it remains only in your head. Have you ever sat down and written a vision for your life for the next forty years—with the years listed? "Here is what I want to do by the year 2009 and 2020 and 2025 and 2048..."

In my office, I have put my whole life in a three-ring binder. Based on my vision, I have to live to be 97. That is why I cannot die any sooner. Death and I have a date.

The first-century leader apostle Paul of Tarsus had a deep sense of his life and his purpose for his generation and mankind. He spoke of completing his work and being ready to die as a natural part of life. He expressed this in a letter to his mentee, a young man named Timothy:

2 Tim 4:6–7 kjv
6 For I am now ready to be offered, and the time of my departure is at hand.
7 I have fought a good fight, I have finished my course, I have kept the faith.

Christ says, "My time is not yet."

John 7:6 kjv
Then Jesus said unto them, My time is not yet come: but your time is always ready.

You have to know when your time is. If you do not know your purpose and your assignment, death will sneak up on you.

Document Your Vision

That is what God did. The Bible is God's written document of His vision. From beginning to end, God knows the end. He knows what it will be like. It is already on paper. How about your vision? Have you written it down?

If you do not write things down, it is as if they never happened. Civilization did not move forward very far until we learned to write things down. The difference between pre-historic and historic time is that we learned to write and humanity used this skill to document and communicate with each other what we were doing here on earth. Writing is essential, not only because it serves to remind you, but it records and documents what happened so others can learn.

William Still was a visionary leader who understood this. He was a black man born free in the northern United States, the son of a man whose father had bought his own freedom from slavery and a mother who stole freedom for herself and some of her children. He grew up to work for an anti-slavery society in Philadelphia and eventually envisioned and carried out, along with his many associates, an effective system of safe houses, guides, and transport that formed the backbone of the system we know as the Underground Railroad, bringing nearly eight hundred souls to freedom.

Although others like Harriet Tubman, as well as many white abolitionists, were active in and often better known for this work, Still's vision included *keeping and publishing a record*. To this day, it remains invaluable to understanding the history of aid to the liberated. He documented the vision.

Write your vision down, because your vision is what gives you power in life to become important, essential, and valuable.

Vision is not a mission; they are different. Most people confuse the two. A mission is a broad general statement about what you wish to accomplish. The mission is essentially a philosophical statement that undergirds the heart of your actions. A written mission statement defines the purpose and justification for your personal, corporate existence.

The key words here are:

General
Philosophical
Justification

A mission statement deals with a general concept of what you want to accomplish. It states your philosophy, your beliefs, and then it justifies your existence.

Vision is opposite to that.

A case in point: McDonald's, Burger King, Pizza Hut, Wendy's,

Denny's, Kentucky Fried Chicken all provide fast food. They all have the same mission. Churches are like that. They have one mission, but they do not all see it that way.

Every church has the same mission. Ask a pastor, "What is your vision?" And the pastor might say, "To win the lost at any cost."

But every church is supposed to win the lost at any cost. That is a mission, not a vision, and that is why a church only has twenty people. People are attracted to vision, not to mission.

Ask another pastor, "What is your vision?"

"Well, to win the city for Jesus." That is not a vision; it is another mission. Jesus said everyone should go and win the world and the city for Him. That is general. That is the co–"mission." The commission. "Go into all the world and preach the gospel." "Co" means together; "mission" means general assignment. Leadership is born when vision is captured, and without it, all activity is simply the management of goals.

The Characteristics of Vision

Vision is a product of a clear sense of purpose and a deep inspiration. Vision is detailed, customized, distinctive, unique, and reasonable. Every word is power packed. I could teach an hour on each word or write pages on it because all of them are very important, but here is the short version.

Vision is the capacity to see beyond your eyes. It is a conceptual manifestation of purpose in pictures. Vision is a glimpse of the future in Technicolor.

Vision is detailed: vision is a conceptual view of the future in such detail that the leader can visit the future, explore its varied components and return to the present and communicate that future in fine description.

Vision is customized: vision is specific to the individual and is the leader's response to a need in his or her environment. The vision is a fit for the leader and separates him or her from other leaders.

Vision is unique: true vision is a tailor-made revelation of a future that gives the leader a picture of hope that becomes his source of inspiration. Vision is a divine assignment that provides a unique view of the world in a preferred future state.

Vision is distinctive: the unique and customized nature of true vision distinguishes it from other visions and places the leader in a preferred position.

Vision is reasonable: although vision may be a lofty conceptual view of the future that stretches the imagination and breaks the boundaries of experiences and the familiar, it is always possible.

Vision is what makes a leader a leader and engenders confidence, trust, dedication, and commitment from others. Without it, there is no leadership, only management.

The Dynamics of Vision

Vision begins to make things happen in the life of a leader and in the workings of a group. It takes on a life of its own, grooming the leader and shaping the mission.

Vision never maintains the status quo. If you have a vision for your life, you have to break out of the status quo, the present condition. Vision is what separates you from the norm.

Vision demands change. It has a preferred future. Once you have captured a vision for your organization or your personal life or your church or your business, you will find that you have to change. Sometimes you have to change companies and change friends because the old ones no longer fit into your vision or they might hamper you from accomplishing it. You are not in the right environment to carry out your vision.

Vision creates self-discipline. It is your vision that disciplines you. If you know where you are going, you know where you do not want to go. Young girls get pregnant and drop out of school because they have no vision of a future that is different. Young men join gangs and commit crimes because too often they have no vision of a future at all. Yet many other young people survive life in urban ghettos and go on to succeed because they know where they do *not* want to go. They see it all around them. They have a vision of where they want to end up. Vision makes self-discipline easier. Such inner discipline involves imposing standards on yourself, and it is the toughest thing in the world. If you know where you are going, however, you can stay on the roadway.

Vision is future focused. It makes you narrow minded, and it is OK to be narrow minded with vision. Leaders have tunnel vision. They keep seeing one thing as they go after it. That is why people with vision have the ability to say no. Sometimes that insults people, but vision keeps the visionary disciplined. "Just say no," as an American anti-drug campaign used to say. "No" to having your time wasted. "No" to giving up on your vision. "No" to moral temptation that would take you off course.

Vision is inspired by God. It is the direct result of godly inspiration. It is the breath of God, as you recall from Chapter 13. It is as if you are an empty balloon. Your life is shapeless, without form, when God takes hold of you and breathes into you the gifts, the purpose, and the vision He has. He breathes the stuff of leadership into you. You become stuffed—inflated—with the things God puts in you. Vision fills your whole life with the right stuff, like the astronaut movie. You are inflated with the will of God. When you have vision, you begin to understand what the Creator placed inside you.

David L. Steward, chairman of the board for World Wide Technology Inc., says people laughed at him in 1990 when he revealed his plans to start a company to provide advanced technological solutions for industry. No one laughs anymore. The company, based in Saint Louis, Missouri, has surpassed $2 billion in sales and has become a major international player. The company is considered to be one of the largest African American–owned businesses in the United States. Its philosophy, Steward says, is, "I try to encourage people that all things are possible through Christ who strengthens us. We've been consistently trying to do the right thing in serving people and putting their best interest first."

He had a purpose in mind that would benefit others. He had godly inspiration, and his servant leadership brought him success. But first, he had a vision.

What Do You Want for Lunch?

The owner of McDonald's on our island of the Bahamas called one day to say, "Pastor Myles, I want to take you for lunch. I want to talk to you about some things. I need some advice." So we went for lunch. He came to pick me up, and I am thinking, "This guy owns McDonald's chain restaurants. I know what we are having for lunch. I am going to get a free McDonald's lunch today; I can order anything I want, man. I'm with the owner."

He headed to a retail area where McDonald's, Burger King, and Kentucky Fried Chicken are located. He drove past McDonald's, and I said, "Where are you going?"

He said, "We are going for lunch."

I said, "But isn't that…"

He said, "Yeah, I know it, that's our place, but I don't feel like eating McDonald's, I feel like eating chicken."

We went right next door to Kentucky Fried Chicken. We walked inside, and the franchise owner met us at the door. Of course, the owners knew each other because they were in the same business, and they greeted each other. I watched them hug each other. The owner welcomed us, shook my hand, and gave us a good seat. He said, "What do you want?" He took our order and put before us everything we wanted and we ate.

Now I was intrigued by this, and I started to ask questions. "Why did you come here?"

He said, "I told you, I want to eat Kentucky Fried Chicken."

I said, "But why didn't you go to your own place?"

He said, "Because I wanted to eat *Kentucky Fried Chicken*."

McDonald's does not sell Kentucky Fried Chicken. A Big Mac will not satisfy the hunger for Kentucky Fried Chicken. Even the owner of McDonald's goes next door if he wants KFC. He wants something unique today that only the Colonel has. McDonald's and Kentucky Fried Chicken have different visions. They know a taste for one cannot be satisfied by the other.

Every gift and divine assignment is designed to meet the needs of a specific market. Not everyone is your market. You will attract the market in keeping with your assignment and gift. Your market will find you.

In our organization in the Bahamas, BFM International, we are identified as "the leadership organization." As an organization, we are synonymous with the words *leadership, purpose, destiny,* and *kingdom,* because these have become the watchwords of our corporate vision and mission. Just as McDonald's and Burger King do not cater to the fine-dining, evening-tuxedo market, we in our organization know that not everybody is attracted to us. The vision of our major organization is "transforming followers into leaders, and leaders into agents of change." Therefore, those who desire to discover, develop, and refine their leadership potential are the ones who come to us from all over the world.

16

Integrity: Protecting Your Gift

"Never let Your Leadership Gift take you where your Character cannot keep you."

Integrity is the manifestation of character, which is oneness of self. Integrity and character are the protectors of leadership and the preservers of vision. Integrity is the essential prerequisite for successful leadership.

The past few years have not been good for those who have been looking to leaders to guide them through the alternatives of daily living. We trust leaders to be examples. Many leaders could not themselves navigate the temptations of life.

Just a few names remind us of the reality of this fact—names like President Bill Clinton, televangelists Jimmy Swaggart and Jim Baker, celebrity entrepreneur Martha Stewart, the Enron Corporation chiefs, and more recently, mega church leader Ted Haggard. Each has been at the center of scandals. Whether it is politics, religion, corporate business, sports, entertainment, or medicine, defects in leadership occur too often.

Let us look at an example of character. There is a lady downtown in the center of the capital city of my country, Nassau, in the Bahamas. I always know where she is, what she is wearing, what she is doing, what she will say, how she feels about everything, and what she is holding in her hand. This lady's name is Victoria, Queen Victoria, that is. She has been sitting in the same chair all my life, and she has never moved. As a child, I remember resting under her shadow from the hot Bahamas sun during the parades and watching her stare at me without saying a word. I remember talking to her and calling her names, but she just looked at me and smiled. All my life, I wondered what she was thinking, but she just sits there and smiles.

What has amazed me about Queen Victoria is that she just sat through the fierce winds and driving rain of the major hurricanes that have hit the islands of our nation, smiling, never reacting to them. The ninety-degree heat of our Bahamas summer sun never makes her sweat. When the pigeons and other birds use her head as a resting place in route to their destination and decide to release themselves on her body, she just sits and smiles. She never yields to temptation.

Victoria is a statue. Statues are intriguing. As I studied Queen Victoria, I realized that she was teaching me one of the greatest lessons of my life, especially as a growing leader. In fact, I have concluded that she has taught me the greatest practical prerequisite for leadership—character.

Cracks in the Wall of Character

Throughout the pages of recorded history, in the wake of human development and civilization, are scattered the sad stories of great men and women who rose to impressive positions of leadership influence. They exercised skill, courage, bravery, expertise, passion, power, vision and charisma, a sense of purpose, faith, resilience, commitment, dedication, and all the other qualities and characteristics we admire in all leaders. Yet most of them failed in the most common area of human experience, the area of character.

Among biblical leaders, Abraham succumbed to the compromise of his wife, Moses lost control of his temper, Saul became a victim of his jealousy, King David surrendered to his lust, Samson laid his strength at the feet of beauty, and Solomon used his influence to indulge his passions. What is the common denominator among all of these leaders? A character defect.

I am convinced that the future of leadership will be determined by the return to character as the priority. Over the past few years, much of the focus of leadership, both in formal and informal training, has been on titles, power, position, skills, gifts, talent, education, charisma, personality, and management competence. It is as if reputation has become more important than personal responsibility and position more than disposition. We need leaders with character.

What is character? The foundational concept of the word *character* is from four principles: fixed, predictable, image, and statue. It implies something that is unchanging and firm. Fixed means it is stable and set; predictable means it can be trusted and sustain expectations; image means its nature is inherent and reflects its essence. Integrity is from the root meaning "integrated" or to be "one."

In other words, having character and integrity means having an integrated self. Who you are, what you say, what you do, and how you appear are all one. It means there is no dichotomy or division in your person. You are not one thing in public and another in private. You are the same in the dark as you are in the light. Character is present in what you say, and what you do is who you are. This is the missing ingredient in leadership today and must be restored to the position of number-one priority. Most of our leaders seem to *be* characters but have none.

Queen Victoria demonstrates the difference between "being a character" and "having character." Character is what you do when no one is watching or what you would do if no one would ever find out. Victoria is the same all night as she is all day.

This is the very nature of God himself. He possesses ultimate character. He boasts that He never changes and is always the same. This is why we can trust Him—He is predictable. He is always there.

"Stop Sinning"

I challenge and admonish every leader who enters my circle of influence to pursue this vital life-protecting, vision-protecting, people-protecting, purpose-protecting principle of leadership. Character is the principle that protects your purpose and potential.

May all leaders be like Victoria and develop the qualities of a statue who does not react or succumb to the external elements or internal voices that attempt to lure us away from the spiritual anchors of the Holy One in whose image we were sculpted.

Here is some good advice for leaders from another leader who kept his character intact. The first-century apostle Paul, speaking of this vital leadership quality, states:

1 Corinthians 15:33–34
33 Do not be misled: "Bad company corrupts good character."
34 Come back to your senses as you ought, and stop sinning; for there are some who are ignorant of God — I say this to your shame.

Romans 5:3–5
3 Not only so, but we also rejoice in our sufferings, because we know that suffering produces perseverance;
4 perseverance, character; and character, hope.
5 And hope does not disappoint us.

It is important to note that character is developed through tests, pressure, and challenges. Face the temptations and challenges like a statue and respond only to the Sculptor. Make character your priority. I challenge and encourage you as a leader to commit yourself to making the cultivation and development of your character your major priority and be an example of one whose integrity can endure to the end.

Among daring, visionary leaders today whom I admire is Lee Iacocca, the top executive who revived Chrysler in the 1980s. He stands out because of his tenacity, his willingness to confront tradition and shake up the old ways of doing things, his ability to make people feel important, and yet at the same time to restructure them in their areas of strength, to be willing to be considered a rebel when in fact he was a revolutionary. I saw those admirable traits in him. To go into an organization and change it from the ground up, while salvaging the value of the people, is incredible servant leadership. He saved people's jobs, and he created products that benefited many, saving fuel and making cars that served the needs of families. This generation needs what he has to offer.

You Are Right on Time

It is important to know that you are not a mistake. Your life is not an experiment with God, but rather an intentional program. It is important to know you are so valuable God would not let you be conceived in your mother's womb unless you were already finished in His mind. God did not choose you recently, and you are not a choice of your parents.

The Bible says God chose you "in him." When? "Before the creation of the world." You existed before you manifested.

Ephesians 1:4–5
4 For he chose us in him before the creation of the world to be holy and blameless in his sight. In love
5 he predestined us to be adopted as his sons through Jesus Christ, in accordance with his pleasure and will.

What is amazing about God is that He timed your entrance. He also chose you in Him, according to the vision of Him that works everything out through the plan of His purpose. He chose you according to the plan He had for your life. "In him we were also chosen, having been predestined according to the plan of him who works out everything in conformity with the purpose of his will" (*Ephesians 1:11*).

You are not one in a million. You are one in millions. He chose you before He made the earth. God timed your arrival on earth. To everything, there is a season, and to every purpose, there is a time. There is a time for purpose.

Ecclesiastes 3:1–2
1 There is a time for everything, and a season for every activity under heaven:
2 a time to be born and a time to die, a time to plant and a time to uproot.

Now, you were born for a purpose, and the purpose was already finished. God gave you breath to start it, but He timed your arrival. Whatever you were born to do, is needed in this generation. There is "a time to be born." Whatever you were born to do is supposed to happen in this generation, this time that you are on earth.

You are destined at this particular time to change the atmosphere of your city, your home, your business, or your church. Purpose is timed. Your birth was timed. Some of your parents might have said to you, "We did not expect you, but you were right on time." Some of you think that you are a mistake, but you are an appointment. God had a vision. You have what this generation needs now. You need what I have. I need what you have. In this generation, whatever you were born to do, we need it now. Maintain your integrity to do it!

If you do not have the character to do what you were born to do, you could be guilty of generational robbery by allowing your gift to remain latent and dormant.

You will experience a whole lot of internal and external opposition. God says, "My purpose will stand."

Proverbs 19:21
Many are the plans in a man's heart, but it is the Lord's purpose that prevails.

You just stay steady. We will get to where you will be established. No one can stop what you were born to do. You are earmarked for success. Go to the end of your dreams. God's idea for you in His kingdom is for you to fulfill your vision in His kingdom.

I encourage you to go back and be a child today—teachable, struggling to be obedient. Children still have a desire to please their parents. Pick up your dreams that you threw away, and say, "Yes, I heard God. I will go back and do what I was born to do. I will become who God gave me breath to be. I am unstoppable."

Your Caravan Is on the Way

I went to Egypt a few years ago with my wife, Ruth. Our hosts took us to the pit that Joseph's brothers threw him in.

When your enemies or your brothers put you in a pit, do not lose your integrity.

Your job may have put you in the pit. Your family may put you in a pit. God says, "Don't move. A caravan is coming to pick you up. Stay steady."

God will shake you up to move you from your comfort zone and put you in a pit to take you to your purpose in life. When you go through some tough times down in the pit, God is preparing your character for your promotion.

Sometimes you feel stuck in a pit, and nothing is working out. You try and nothing works. You feel depressed. You begin to think that God forgot you. God says, "No, there's a caravan coming to pick you up and take you to your next purpose."

When Joseph was down in the pit, he knew this was not the vision he had. When his brothers sold him to traders in the caravan, he thought, "This was not in my dream."

I imagine that Joseph did not cry in the pit. He did not get mad at God or complain in the pit. He just sat in the pit, thinking, "This is not what I saw, so it has to be temporary." Whatever "pit" you are going through is temporary.

Purpose is more important than a pit. Purpose is more powerful than a pit. Stay in the pit for now if you have to, because God put you there for a reason; He is coming to get you when it is time. He will take you to your destination, if you maintain your integrity.

When the caravan came and Joseph's brothers sold him, they thought they were selling him into slavery. It was an excursion to his purpose—all expenses paid. Think of Joseph staggering behind a camel in the hot desert sun, walking in camel dung, walking in the heat. His brothers sold him into slavery, but he was on his way to the throne to become Pharaoh's right-hand man.

Genesis 41:41
So Pharaoh said to Joseph, "I hereby put you in charge of the whole land of Egypt."

Even when you are staggering, wondering what is about to happen, God says, "Just hold to the rope, I am taking you to your throne."

Your vision is bigger than this! What God called you to do is bigger than this! The pit is not the end.

There did come a time when Joseph's family had to come to him for food:

Genesis 42:6
Now Joseph was the governor of the land, the one who sold grain to all its people. So when Joseph's brothers arrived, they bowed down to him with their faces to the ground.

Some of you feel imprisoned in your employment. God said, "That's OK. Don't get mad." Do what Joseph did—don't get mad; maximize the moment.

You are great. No one knows you yet. People think they know who you are, but on the inside of you is a leader they have not seen yet. Even your parents or your spouse has not seen the leader you have inside of you. You are still on your way to your end. They do not know who you are.

Should you maintain your integrity, no one can stop what you were born to do. So stay steady, stay committed, and stay focused. You are in your leadership spot. You have your assignment. You are secure in your area of gifting. The place is prepared for you. Be about the Father's business, with excellent character.

17

Train: Who Will Come After You?

L eadership is mentoring! Identifying, developing, training, and preparing your replacements as a leader is one of your primary contributions to the world.

Imagine your boss promoted you and came into your office the day you started working in your new position and said, "Congratulations! You are a servant leader now. You are in your leadership spot, pursuing the vision and carrying out the plan. You really seem to know your purpose, and you have an extraordinary gift in this arena of leadership. Don't get comfortable, though. It is time to start preparing your successors."

"But I just got here," you might respond. "I don't want people to think they can replace *me*—take over my job." At the same time, you might be thinking, "I know she's crazy if she thinks I am going to train my competition."

If so, you are not yet a true leader.

It is time to graduate.

The marks of true leadership include these:

True leaders do not maintain followers. They produce leaders. Insecure leaders with poor self-esteem are afraid to develop people. They need dependent followers to prop them up. These are not leaders.

True leaders believe that leadership potential resides in everyone around them. They create an environment for that leadership to blossom. The heart of a true leader is not just serving one's gift, but also helping other people to find their prepared places, to discover their gifts and strengths, and to give them an opportunity to develop.

True leaders create an environment for others to find their authority. You have authority in your area of gifting. My job as an authority is to help you find your area of authority, so you can go and serve the world.

Authorizing a Transition

That is just what Jesus did. The earthbound Leader succeeded in His mission, then left, sending out His authorized successors — putting them in charge of the global initiative to communicate the Good News.

This sets an example for us and demonstrates some truths about preparing others to lead:

Servant leaders produce servant leaders.

A leader inspires others to become leaders and fulfill their own purposes. In essence, true leadership success is measured by the diminishing dependence of your followers. Colleagues will need the leader less, be less dependent, if the leader is doing a good job. If your staff, congregation, or family can function well when you are not around, you are an effective leader. If they can carry on even after you have retired, resigned, or gone to Glory, you have fulfilled your mission. Leadership effectiveness is measured not by what happens in your presence but by what happens in your absence.

If your household dissolved in chaos every time you went out on an errand, or worse, your family disintegrated upon your death and never recovered, something was wrong with your leadership. The test of a leader is how many others are leading—or at least trained to lead.

Success produces successors.

The disciples had been the trainees of Jesus for three years, following Him around, listening to everything He had to say, and assisting in His ministry. His death came as a terrible blow to them. The hours between His death and the revelation of His resurrection must have been devastatingly depressing and terrifying. Someone might be coming for them next. Yet, if the disciples had remained scattered in silent exile after the Crucifixion or huddled in fear and never emerged from the mountain where Matthew says the risen Jesus revealed Himself, Christ's mission would have ended in failure. His message would never have gotten out. We might be colonized subjects of pagan Rome today, Jews still waiting for the Messiah or otherwise oblivious to Christ's teachings.

Matthew 28: 5–7

5 The angel said to the women, "Do not be afraid, for I know that you are looking for Jesus, who was crucified.

6 He is not here; he has risen, just as he said. Come and see the place where he lay.

7 Then go quickly and tell his disciples: 'He has risen from the dead and is going ahead of you into Galilee. There you will see him.' Now I have told you."

Matthew 28:16–19

16 Then the eleven disciples went to Galilee, to the mountain where Jesus had told them to go.

17 When they saw him, they worshiped him; but some doubted.

18 Then Jesus came to them and said, "All authority in heaven and on earth has been given to me.

19 Therefore go and make disciples of all nations, baptizing them in the name of the Father and of the Son and of the Holy Spirit."

Jesus says, "All authority is given to *Me*."

He adds, "In heaven and earth."

He says, "Therefore, [*you*] go and make disciples…"

That is what is essential to understand here. The reason God gives us authority is not to use it on people but to release people.

In this encounter, He is the resurrected Savior, back from the dead. He went to hell, picked up some keys, rose again. He is on the back side of the cross. He is victorious over death, hell, and the grave. He is powerful in all of His glory, and He is now ready to take on the world, declaring, "All authority in heaven and in earth has now been given unto Me."

He said, basically, "I have authority; therefore, you go and be in authority in your area of gifting, in your prepared spot." He gave us authority not so that we can use it on people, but to release people into the purposes for which the Creator made them. He was saying, in effect, "I have authority; therefore, you go and be yourself; fulfill your calling and find your leadership spot."

At the Passover meal (the Last Supper), after instructing His Seder companions on servant leadership and warning of His impending betrayal, the rabbi Jesus handed over a kingdom:

Luke 22:28–30
28 You are those who have stood by me in my trials.
29 And I confer on you a kingdom, just as my Father conferred one on me,
30 so that you may eat and drink at my table in my kingdom and sit on thrones, judging the twelve tribes of Israel.

This is a vital point that many do not realize: oppressing or suppressing others leads to loss for both the oppressor and the oppressed, because the oppressor can never benefit from the true gifts of those he is oppressing. I observed this firsthand once when I traveled to South Africa. There was poverty everywhere, and the wealth of the land was in the hands of only 4 percent of the population. The potential of multitudes of people was wasted, and they were living in cardboard boxes. I looked at it and just wept. South Africa had squandered the talents and gifts of so many, robbing itself of their potential. I have made it a personal mission to go back to South Africa as often as possible to help develop leaders there.

Oppression destroys gifts. South Africa could not benefit from the many and splendid gifts of those it held down, ignored, and oppressed until leaders dismantled apartheid. Germany could not benefit from the enormous gifts and contributions of the people Hitler destroyed. Slaveholding nations like the United States and Brazil could not fully benefit from the tremendous potential of the Africans while they held them in bondage. The Soviet Union could not benefit from the stunted, untapped gifts of its own people while it ruled with an iron fist.

Put another way, the true purpose for authority is to release other people's authority, not to control it.

True authority releases more authority.

The true joy for leaders is not to see others serve them—"You are not to be like that"—but to see others discover themselves. "But you are not to be like that. Instead, the greatest among you should be like the youngest, and the one who rules like the one who serves" (*Luke* 22:26). The leader knows that if others merely follow him, he cannot benefit from their gifts. If others find their gifts and serve them to the world, it will improve his life as well, and he can benefit from them.

Self-centered leadership produces self-centered followers.

Maybe this is the problem with most leaders in the world today. We are seeing more people who are self-centered, who are motivated for self-promotion or motivated by financial gain and looking out for Number One, rather than by the desire to serve.

Sometimes friends treat you differently when they get into a position of power. And when some people receive authority, it goes to their heads. Instead of using it to help people, they use it to keep people down, to oppress people, to make sure others do not compete with them. Competition for positions of power is evidence of insecurity. If the leaders were secure in their positions and confident of their visions, their gifts, and their assignments, they would not need to worry. On that final night with Jesus, you recall, the disciples argued again over which one was the greatest (see *Luke 22:24*).

In teaching leadership, I have discovered a lot about myself and how to be God-centered, rather than self-centered. In my organization, we develop potential. Every human being possesses potential. I have to keep testing my leadership by leaving. That manifests other people's gifts. To develop leaders I have to be secure in my own leadership. Insecurity is what prevents people from mentoring. If you have a clear conviction regarding your own value as a leader, then your greatest joy will be to help others discover theirs and give them room to execute and manifest it. You will have no place for jealousy, fear, suspicion, and other emotions that are so pervasive in traditional leadership, where people jockey and fight for position, afraid of someone taking their place.

As a leader, I realize that you and I are equal before God. My goal is to try to bring you up and push you up beyond where I am, because I want to find the gift that you are supposed to serve to me. You respect my gift. I respect your gift.

The Next Generation

When people come in to see our staff work at our organization in the Bahamas, they find a spirit of responsibility, self-motivation, and purpose. Our people are excited and highly motivated.

We do a lot of work with young people to develop leadership. My conviction is if we can get the youth to understand the concept of leadership, then the future is secure. Teaching leadership begins at home. Parents must prepare their children to carry on, to take up leadership in the next generation.

The Kennedy family is a good example of that. For generations, it has suffered the loss of its leaders: Joseph Sr., Joseph Jr., John, Robert, John Jr., Rose. As blessed as it was with material things, the family suffered many tragedies. All the while, it kept a high profile in public service. In each generation, someone seems to step to the forefront, and the family's legacy, influence, and leadership goes on.

In recent times, it seems the role has fallen to Caroline, the daughter of President John F. Kennedy, especially after the death of her brother, John Jr. In a similar manner, Edward "Teddy" Kennedy had to step up following the death of his brothers, John and Robert, in relatively quick succession.

Despite deaths, setbacks, and scandals, the family always seems to have trained someone in the next generation in their values of faith, philanthropy, and government service—their gifts of servant leadership.

When my own children, Charissa and Charo, were growing up, I paid them to read my books and encouraged them to become leaders. Now they are becoming real leaders. Both of them are compassionate people, and I think that is generational. My wife and I are living what we learned from our parents—to serve others—and I anticipate that our children will be greater servants than we are.

My daughter's choice of career is social work, and I am astonished at her empathy for people. She was considering going into medicine and had jobs at a local hospital on the island from the time she was a teenager. Later, she decided, "No, I would rather be among the people than just working on a body." She is working on a doctorate and has a job with a community organization in Texas. I hear stories about her and how, at age 24, she is touching lives.

My son, Charo, who has been in graduate school in the United States, wants to go into business. I asked him, "Why do you want to go into business." He said, "So I can make money to help people." His motivation again is probably the same one I had when I was his age. It is good to hear a young man at age 23 say, "I want to generate resources—not to buy a boat or a big car—but rather to serve people." It is very fulfilling to hear that.

*   *   *

I cannot overemphasize that both male and female are born to lead equally. Even though they are different, different does not mean that one is inferior or superior. Different means unique. We train both genders male and female with the same conviction that everyone has a gift. We do not discriminate.

Nor do we deal with any leadership experiences based on race. We believe that all humanity has equal value. We are all parts of one body, as Paul puts it in his first Letter to the Corinthians:

1 Corinthians 12:14–20
14 Now the body is not made up of one part but of many.
15 If the foot should say, "Because I am not a hand, I do not belong to the body," it would not for that reason cease to be part of the body.
16 And if the ear should say, "Because I am not an eye, I do not belong to the body," it would not for that reason cease to be part of the body.
17 If the whole body were an eye, where would the sense of hearing be? If the whole body were an ear, where would the sense of smell be?
18 But in fact God has arranged the parts in the body, every one of them, just as he wanted them to be.
19 If they were all one part, where would the body be?
20 As it is, there are many parts, but one body.

An example of the impact that leaders can have on those who come after is Mother Teresa, who founded a religious order, the Missionaries of Charity, and won the Nobel Peace Prize in 1979 for her work among the destitute. I do not think Mother Teresa wanted to start an order of sisters per se. She was trying to help the lepers and others who were downtrodden in Calcutta. "Of free choice, my God, and out of love for you, I desire to remain and do whatever be your Holy will in my regard," she once said.

Yet she inspired those who worked with her to follow her example, even to dress like her. Pope John Paul II, presiding over her beatification by the Roman Catholic Church in 2003 called her "one of the greatest missionaries of the twentieth century."

We need more missionaries like her who spawn other missionaries, leaders who make leaders.

Leading for Succession

True leadership provides the resources, policies, and assistance to help people discover their gifts. Look at the failure of Communism; it could not work even though it preaches equality. It still resulted in the elite versus the masses. The masses were not motivated to work because the system did not allow them to exercise their gifts. They were commanded to do what the state said. That worked against personal development. Poverty, low self-esteem, lack of incentive, lack of entre-preneurial spirit—all of these are products of any culture that does not encourage people to discover their personal leadership.

If leaders provide an environment that encourages people to discover their own gifts, everybody benefits. No one is just a servant, and everybody is a leader who serves a gift to others. The economy becomes powerful and strong because small businesses are the strength of economic growth. Entrepreneurship enables people to discover their gift of leadership.

Governments often fail to plan for their succession. I have had the privilege of meeting many leaders. I have sat with the president of Israel. I have received one of the highest honors from the queen of England, called the Order of the British Empire (OBE) award. I have been the guest of the Queen Mother and the king of Swaziland. I have had the opportunity to sit with Nelson Mandela as president of South Africa. I have advised and dined with the president of Namibia. I have slept in the house of the president of Zambia.

From all of these wonderful experiences, I have concluded that the aspect of leadership that is most lacking is training for succession.

Eighty percent of all leadership conflict in the developing countries takes place at transition, either at the death of a leader or because of a coup. Conflict comes whenever there is a change in leadership in an organization or a political party. It is the same in the so-called developed nations. Even the election process of democracies is a messy business. I have sat down to eat with renowned religious and corporate leaders. I have had the opportunity to sit with civic leaders and serve with some of them. Failure to plan for succession is common to all, as well as in churches, nonprofit organizations, and schools.

The Principles of Leadership Transfer

Nothing is more difficult than transition in leadership. We keep making the same mistakes, because we do not understand the principles of leadership transfer. Let us look at some principles.

Leadership is never given to just one generation. If you grasp that concept, suddenly you realize that every leader is temporary. Sometimes our greatest temptation or weakness as leaders is to think that the world begins and ends with us. Leadership is always transitional. Any leader who thinks that he or she is permanent will face one neutralizing agent—death. No matter how terrorizing or wonderful a leader may be, death will eventually terminate them. It is important to keep your mortality constantly in your mind as a leader.

Leadership that serves only its generation is destined for failure. You should never lead with only your generation in mind. Whether you are a Sunday school teacher, a teacher in a public-school classroom or a company executive responsible for an entire department, remember that your responsibility is to not only serve your generation but also provide for the future.

God is a generational God. God always addresses the unborn. God acts generationally. Leadership that is genuine, that is from God, always thinks generationally.

Success without a successor is failure. It does not matter how successful you are as a leader. If you have no successor, it does not matter how much people may talk about the great things you have accomplished and the good things you have done. You have been a failure. **If your business, your ministry, or your vision dies with you, you failed.** It does not matter how great your vision is. It does not matter how great your ideas about your company, ministry, country, or church may be. If, when you die, it all dies, you were a failure. A vision that is genuinely from God will always be bigger than your lifetime. So do not ever attempt to complete your vision in your lifetime. God is too big for that. He will always give you a vision that will outlive you. A part of your responsibility as a visionary is to prepare your replacement to continue the work. If your work dies when you die, you have failed. Many people have done work on earth that people admired and that benefited people while they were living, but they failed if they took to the cemetery everything that they were supposed to leave with us.

The Final Class

The average leader employs other people. The true leader deploys other people.

I do not want employees in my company. I am after "deploy-ees." I have to create an environment in which they can deploy their gifts and serve their gifts to the world. I do not want to control people; I want to release people. That is why Christ says in effect, "I have authority in heaven and the earth and under the earth and because I have all the authority in all these areas, *you* go and release yours."

True leaders are not afraid of the success of their followers. If you become nervous when people around you succeed, you are not a true leader. You are a manipulator; you are insecure. Leaders who are serving their gifts to the world, who have attracted and inspired people, who know they are not here forever, get their replacements up to speed.

Train your successor. Teach them everything you know about leading your particular kind of endeavor, be it a church or a circus. Help them to refine their gifts, which may be different from yours.

Do not get comfortable. It is time to start preparing your successors.

Jesus chose Peter as the one to build His church (*Matthew 16:18*), but first He had to teach Him to serve:

John 21:17

The third time he said to him, "Simon son of John do you love me?" Peter was hurt because Jesus asked him the third time, "Do you love me?"
He said, "Lord, you know all things; you know that I love you."
Jesus said, "Feed my sheep."

The Lord Jesus, the greatest leader of all time, often taught by showing people what to do. He was a man of action. He demonstrated service. On His final night of freedom, He began washing the feet of His disciples (see *John 13:1–17*).

Later, Jesus asked those whose feet He had washed, if they understood what He was trying to teach and explained that He was being a role model for how He wanted them to act. He served them, so that they would see how they should serve.

John 13:12–17

12 When he had finished washing their feet, he put on his clothes and returned to his place. "Do you understand what I have done for you?" he asked them.
13 "You call me 'Teacher' and 'Lord,' and rightly so, for that is what I am.
14 Now that I, your Lord and Teacher, have washed your feet, you also should wash one another's feet.
15 I have set you an example that you should do as I have done for you.
16 I tell you the truth, no servant is greater than his master, nor is a messenger greater than the one who sent him.
17 Now that you know these things, you will be blessed if you do them.

"Now That You Know..."

Leadership is serving at every opportunity.

The world-famous basketball icon Michael Jordan is a great example of servant leadership. Today, he is considered a leader and generates respect wherever he goes. He is also one of the wealthiest men in the U.S., and his name alone is worth millions. Yet it is amazing that Michael never did set out to become a leader. He simply desired to be himself and to maximize his athletic gift. He became a slave to his gift and served it to us all for years and now we call him "great."

He got to this point because he is a slave. When you and I were sleeping, he was practicing. When we were relaxing, he was jogging. When we were shopping, he was in the gym. When we were watching television, he was shooting baskets for hours. He was a slave to his gift. That is why people seek him out and reward him for the gift he served the world. This is what Jesus meant when He said, in effect, "He who would be great among you must be the slave of all."

Have you found something that you can be a slave to, so you can serve it to the world?

Or, are you looking and waiting for a chance to lead? The opportunities are all around you. Clean the bathroom, dust the floor, hand out books, park cars, be a greeter at church, volunteer at the library, or work at Wal-Mart. Opportunity is what servants seek.

I used to do everything that needed doing at my church: open the building, fix chairs, play the piano, lead the praise team, and then preach afterward. I ran the camera and also the soundboard. I duplicated tapes myself. Now, we have a staff of 60 full-time workers and another 120 to help with ministry, but I used to do everything they do. I used to clean the floor. Whatever I ask others to do, I once did.

One reason leaders do the little things is to prepare themselves. They refine their gifts by serving in all the roles. They gain experience so they can teach the next person exactly how to do it. They can *show* the next generation of leaders, not just tell them or send them a book. It is hard to groom a successor if you came in at the top and never had

to work your way up through the ranks. Go back and be a slave, a servant, the youngest.

Do not look for power. Look for opportunity. True leaders do not
walk into a bathroom, see a piece of paper on the floor, and ask, "Where
is the maintenance man?" No, the piece of paper and the maintenance
of bathroom sanitation become their personal responsibility.

Be the model of responsibility for the next generation. Servant leadership is serving your gift at every opportunity, not only when people
can see you doing it. Be a slave to it, and serve others as you do.

Then, turn it over to the one who loves to serve.

When Jesus Christ was about to change leadership, He called a final
meeting, a breakfast meeting by the Sea of Tiberias. He was in resurrected form. He was ready to change leadership. He called everyone
together for a staff meeting. He was about to identify His successor.

John 21:15–17

*15 When they had finished eating, Jesus said to Simon Peter, "Simon son of John, do
you truly love me more than these?" "Yes, Lord," he said, "you know that I love you."
Jesus said, "Feed my lambs."*

*16 Again Jesus said, "Simon son of John, do you truly love me?" He answered, "Yes,
Lord, you know that I love you." Jesus said, "Take care of my sheep."*

*17 The third time he said to him, "Simon son of John, do you love me?" Peter was
hurt because Jesus asked him the third time, "Do you love me?" He said, "Lord, you
know all things; you know that I love you." Jesus said, "Feed my sheep."*

Jesus the CEO did not say to Simon Peter, "Simon, are you famous?
Are you intelligent? Do you have good personality? Do you have competence, skills, expertise? Do you have experience? Do you love My
vision? Do you like My power? Do you love My mission?"

No! He asks, "Do you love *Me*?" This is the test. "Do you love me, Peter?"

Peter essentially says, "Yes, Lord. Master, You know I love You. I
have been tested." Among other things, Peter had cut off a man's ear to
defend the Master and risked waiting nearby when He was on trial.

Jesus says, in effect, "Then you are in charge. Feed My lambs; you are going to take over the company. Take it to the next level. Go forth and produce leaders."

Review

To review, true leaders:

Know themselves and develop themselves according to their gifting

Declare independence from the expectations and opinions of others

Learn from others, but never copy them

Are more concerned with expressing themselves than proving themselves

Measure leadership not by how many people serve them, but by how many people they serve

Lead others to leadership

Set others free to become leaders, instead of maintaining followers

Create an environment and provide opportunity for others to discover and fulfill their Creator-given purpose and potential

Deploy others, while traditional leaders employ others

Release others into their own unique gifting

Understand that success without a successor is failure

Consider it their own success when those they have empowered can lead others into their own purposes and gifting

Produce leaders who produce other leaders who produce other leaders

Remember and embrace the seven major principles of Servant Leadership and find your spot in the galaxy of humanity.

Leadership is <u>a prepared position.</u>
Leadership <u>demands a price.</u>
Leadership is <u>inherent.</u>
Leadership is <u>a divine deposit.</u>
Leadership is <u>not for you but for others.</u>
Leadership is <u>becoming yourself for the benefit of others.</u>

Go unto *all* the world and produce the leaders that the world needs. Remember the greatest leadership principle and philosophy of all time, wise words from the Leader of all leaders: "Instead, whoever wants to become great among you must be your servant, and whoever wants to be first must be your slave" (*Matthew 20:26–27*).

Leadership is *predetermined and not a preference.*

The world is waiting for your leadership.

> *May the Lord make you increase, both you and your children.*
> *May you be blessed by the Lord, the Maker of heaven and earth.*
> *The highest heavens belong to the Lord, but the earth he has given to man.*
> *It is not the dead who praise the Lord, those who go down to silence;*
> *it is we who extol the Lord, both now and forevermore.*
> Psalm 115:14–18

10 Keys to Becoming a Leader

1. Confirm Your Purpose

Verify the original vision God had for your life. Take everything you thought you were, give it to him and let him show you what you have never seen.

2. Document Your Vision

Visualize your destiny. What plans do you need to make to accomplish it? Who could help you fulfill your purpose while fulfilling their own?

3. Discover Your Potential

Assess your gifts, skills and abilities. Then develop and refine them.

4. Maintain Your Passion

Do this through prayer, nurturing an active desire to see your purpose manifested and being persistent.

5. Earn Trust

Be trustworthy so that others can have confidence in you.

6. Preserve Integrity

Guard your heart and make sure your motives are pure and your actions are in accordance with the nature of the Creator.

7. Establish Values and Principles

Know who you are and for what you stand. Learn discipline and self-management. Know the nature and qualities of a servant leader and practice them.

8. Cultivate the Spirit of Faith

Cultivate a trust in the Creator through prayer and acquaintance with God's Word. Have faith that he will fulfill his purposes for your life so you can be the leader He created you to be.

9. Dare to Explore the Unknown

Explore the dreams, ideas, people and resources you need to serve your gift to the world.

10. Be Yourself by "Serving Yourself"

Practice servant leadership by actively serving your gifts on behalf of those around you. When you cease functioning, you lose your value.

ENDNOTES

Chapter 6 — Who Died and Left You in Charge?: The Dominion Mandate

1. Page 45, James Weldon Johnson, ed. *The Book of American Negro Poetry* (New York: Bartleby, 1922).

Chapter 7 — Jockeying for Position: The Sons of Zebedee

1. Page 62, Mahatma Gandhi, *Gandhi An Autobiography: The Story of My Experiments with Truth,* (Ypsilanti, MI: Beacon Press, 1993).

Chapter 11 — Leaders Are Made, Not Born: Self–Discovery Is the Main Ingredient

1. Page 102, Mahatma Gandhi, *The Essential Gandhi: An Anthology of His Writings on His Life* (New York: Vintage, 2002).